# My Child Has Autism

## What Parents Need to Know

by Clarissa Willis, Ph.D.

**Bulk purchase**

Gryphon House books are available for special premiums and sales promotions as well as for fund-raising use. Special editions or book excerpts also can be created to specification. For details, contact the Director of Marketing at Gryphon House.

**Disclaimer**

Gryphon House, Inc. and the author cannot be held responsible for damage, mishap, or injury incurred during the use of or because of activities in this book. Appropriate and reasonable caution and adult supervision of children involved in activities and corresponding to the age and capability of each child involved, is recommended at all times. Do not leave children unattended at any time. Observe safety and caution at all times.

**Note:** Because three out of four children diagnosed with autism are boys, this book typically uses the male pronoun when discussing children with autism, though does occasionally use the female pronoun, in order to represent the female portion of children who have autism.

# My
# Child
# Has
# Autism

## WHAT PARENTS NEED TO KNOW

# CLARISSA WILLIS, Ph.D.

Illustrated by Deborah Johnson
and Marie Ferrante Doyle

**Gryphon House, Inc.**
**Beltsville, Maryland, USA**

**Library of Congress Cataloging-in-Publication Information**
Willis, Clarissa.
  My child has autism : what parents need to know / by
Clarissa Willis.
     p. cm.
  Includes index.
  ISBN 978-0-87659-093-5
  1.  Autism in children--Popular works.  I. Title.
  RJ506.A9W487 2009
  618.92'85882--dc22
                              2009004706

# Table of Contents

# Introduction

*"When Nathan was created, there was a microscopic change, which occurred randomly in nature. We don't know why it happened, and we didn't cause it to happen...we've always tried to do our best with him, even if it was not what his therapists thought we should be doing. Please remember, Nathan is valued by his family...he is a joy and a gift. In fact, when he was almost a year old, we discovered the name Nathan means 'Gift.'"*

—*Helen Lane, mother of Nathan*

There are no words that adequately describe what happens when parents learn that their child has autism. Some parents feel profound grief, while others struggle to gather as much information as possible. Still other families frantically seek out second, third, and even fourth opinions. Families often go through distinct cycles that range from grief and loss to shopping for a cure and, finally, to an acceptance of what is.

Even with the technological advances in the medical field, we still do not know what causes autism or why it affects boys four times more often than girls. What we do know however, is that one child in every 150 will be diagnosed with autism.

This book is for families of young children with autism spectrum disorder. The information and ideas in this book reflect the author's 30 years of experience as a teacher, speech pathologist, early interventionist, and consultant with children with autism and their families.

Although each child with autism is unique, it is possible to make some generalizations. Most children with autism spectrum disorder will have varying degrees of difficulty with behavior, communication skills, ability to relate to others, and, in some cases, their ability to learn in the same way that typically developing children learn. While there is no cure for autism, there is hope. With structured early intervention, consistent behavior management, and speech and language intervention, many individuals with autism lead productive lives.

Today, many treatments for autism are available. While some of these treatments are under debate, others are based on years of sound scientific research. However, most professionals agree that each child with autism is special and has his or her own set of strengths and weaknesses, and that each child falls somewhere within the spectrum, exhibiting either more or less of certain characteristics. This book will explain autism, discuss the major characteristics associated with autism, and offer some easy-to-use strategies for helping children with autism function in their homes, at school, and in the community.

The following statement sums it up best, "Autism isn't something a person has, or a 'shell' someone is trapped inside. There is no normal child hidden behind the autism.... Autism is a way of being." (Jim Sinclair, 1993)

# Chapter 1

# Putting the Pieces Together to Understand This Puzzle Called Autism

*Autism is a puzzle, you know all the pieces are there, and you just have to figure out a way to put them all together. But once you do it, is exciting to see the whole of it and to know that no matter what happens next you have done your best.*
*—Richard, the father of Brian*

## What Is Autism?

Children with autism have been around long before autism had an official name. In 1943, Leo Kanner first defined autism when he described 11 children with similar characteristics. The following year, Hans Asperger described a group of children with behavior issues. Although they had never met, both men used identical terms to describe the disorder.

The most accepted definition of autism is a person with delayed or typical behaviors in the following categories:

- Interaction with others (socializing),
- Communication (responding to others), and
- Behavior (hand wringing or rocking back and forth, for example).

This definition is from the Diagnostic and Statistical Manual of Mental Disorders, Fourth Edition-Text Revision, or DSM-IV-TR, which is a manual used by the American Psychological Association.

The American Autism Society defines autism as "a complex developmental disability that typically appears during the first three years of life."

With new research and information, we are learning more about diagnosing and treating autism than ever before. Unfortunately, the more that experts learn about autism, the more questions they discover they have about autism that, according to the National Institutes of Health, may affect as many as one in every 500 children.

According to the Center for Disease Control, this disorder may affect as many as one in every 150 children.

Regardless of how autism is defined, you will need the following:

- Up-to-date, accurate information about the primary characteristics of autism;
- A strong support system that includes specialists such as early interventionists, special education teachers, speech pathologists, and occupational therapists;
- A positive relationship with your child's teacher so that together you can share the child's successes and challenges; and

- Information about how to help with your child's behavior, communication skills, social skills, and self-help skills.

# Why Is It Called Autism Spectrum Disorder?

Autism is described as a spectrum disorder because children with autism have characteristics that range from very mild to quite severe. Using the term autism spectrum disorder, or ASD, means a child falls somewhere along that range, or continuum. Because it is a continuum, a child may be at the mild end in terms of ability to learn new skills, and at the severe end in terms of behavior. In this book, *autism* is used to refer to a child who has autism spectrum disorder.

Although each child with autism is unique, specialists generally agree that all children with autism spectrum disorders have difficulty in varying levels of:
- Language and communication,
- Social relationships, and
- Response to sensory stimuli.

In addition, children with autism may display behaviors that are not typical of their peers. For example, many young children with autism have gaps in their development ranging from developing skills out of the typical sequence of acquisition to fixating on particular objects, such as a puzzle or a rotating fan. Parents often describe children with autism as being like pieces of Swiss cheese—there are

Parents often describe children with autism as being like pieces of Swiss cheese—there are gaps or holes in what they learn, how they learn it, and how they respond to their world.

gaps or holes in what they learn, how they learn it, and how they respond to their world.

# What Do I Need to Know About Children with Autism?

While research may lead to new and better techniques for working with children with autism, for now, you want to know:

- What strategies can I use to help my child with everyday activities,
- How can I help him control his behavior, and
- What programs or plans work best so my child can learn to communicate, play, and interact meaningfully with peers?

This book is designed to help you understand autism and plan for the success of your child. The first step is to examine the characteristics of children with autism and learn how children with that characteristic relate to the world around them.

The following chart is a summary of the basic characteristics often associated with autism. The chapters in this book include more information about these characteristics.

## Basic Characteristics of Autism

| Characteristic | How the Child Might Act |
|---|---|
| Undesired Behaviors (Maladaptive) | ■ Constant or repetitive behavior, such as waving hands or hand-flapping<br>■ Hitting self or others<br>■ Tantrums<br>■ Aggressive toward others |
| Lack of Functional Communication | ■ Echolalia<br>■ Stereotypic phrases<br>■ Nonsense speech<br>■ No speech/language |
| Problems with Social Interaction | ■ Only interacts when something is needed<br>■ Interacts with objects, not people<br>■ Preoccupation with things, not people<br>■ Totally in his or her own world |
| Obsessions | ■ Rituals<br>■ Routines that must be followed<br>■ Only eats specific types of foods<br>■ May be obsessed with objects (such as spoons) |

**The most important thing you need to know is that the sooner your child with autism receives sound, consistent, and appropriate services, the better his chance for success. While there is still much to learn about how to reach children with autism and how to help them adapt to a world that is constantly changing, we know that working as a team with other professionals can lead to positive results.**

# Words, Words, Words—Why Is There So Much Autism-Related Jargon?

The words that people use to talk about autism can make it very confusing. With all the responsibilities of parenting a young child, the last thing you need is to carry around a dictionary in order to discuss your child's condition. For example, a speech pathologist tells you that your child needs to stop using *echolalia* and learn to use functional communication. After searching the Internet to decipher what the speech pathologist was referring to, you learn that echolalia is a term that simply means repeating everything that is heard.

This book will help to explain autism without using complicated jargon. When a specific term is used, it will be explained in simple terms. Definitions of key terms are also repeated at the end of each chapter. Most chapters include specific strategies or activities that you can use at home, in the community, and share with your child's teacher. These strategies take very little time and their materials cost almost nothing.

As you broaden your understanding of your child with autism, you may increasingly view him as a special and unique person with talents, strengths, and potential. The following reminders focus on what your child can learn, rather than on behaviors and areas that may be difficult for your child.

**Always put your child first.** Your child is a child with autism, not an autistic child.

**Each child is unique**, and while your child may have characteristics typical of other children with autism, he will have other characteristics that are distinctly his own.

**Look for information about autism from a reliable source** and remember that there may be more than one way to solve a problem. Information, even what you see or hear on television and the Internet, may not come from reliable sources.

**There is no single method, magic pill, or specific program that can "cure" or "fix" autism**. While many programs and methods have been tried and are successful with some children, they may not be successful with others. If a method seems too good to be true or promises a cure for autism, chances are that the person presenting it just wants to sell a product. There may or may not be sound research backing up that product.

# What Are the Major Types of Autism?

Autism-related disorders fall into a single broad category called Pervasive Developmental Delay (PDD), which is sometimes used interchangeably with autism spectrum disorder (ASD). A useful way to consider PDD/ASD is to think of them as different branches growing from the trunk of one tree. Each branch, though slightly different from the other branches, is still part of the tree. The same is true of the various types of autism.

The recognized types of autism spectrum disorder include:
- Autism,
- Pervasive Developmental Disorder Not Otherwise Specified (PDDNOS),
- Asperger's Syndrome,
- Rett's Syndrome, and
- Childhood Disintegrative Disorder (Heller's Syndrome).

## Autism

To be diagnosed with autism, a child must exhibit a significant number of the following characteristics:

- A significant delay in social interaction, such as eye contact or facial expression;
- A communication delay;
- Behaviors including stereotypical behavior, such as intense, almost obsessive, preoccupation with objects;
- The need for routines that are nonfunctional and ritualistic, such as lining up all the books or food in a certain manner; and
- Repeating motor movements over and over, such as finger-popping or hand-flapping.

## Pervasive Developmental Disorder Not Otherwise Specified (PDDNOS)

This classification is used when a child has autism, yet the characteristics the child displays are not like the characteristics of other children with autism. This diagnosis is also used when the onset of the disorder happens after age three. Of all the autism classifications, used for autism, this is the most vague and confusing. However, this allows specialists to classify a child as having autism when he displays a few, but not all, of the characteristics of autism. This makes it possible for the child to receive the needed services.

## Asperger's Syndrome

Children with Asperger's Syndrome traditionally behave much like children with other types of autism when they are young, in that they have some difficulty with communication, social interaction, and/or behaviors. However, as they grow into middle school age or in adolescence, children with

Asperger's often learn how to socialize, communicate, and behave in a more socially acceptable manner. Most children with Asperger's have normal or above-normal intelligence, so they learn new skills as fast as, or, in many cases, faster than their peers without autism. These children have been described as having difficulty with coordination, vocal tone (they tend to speak in a monotone), depression, violent reactions to change, and they have a tendency for ritualistic behaviors. In addition, children with Asperger's Syndrome may develop intense obsessions with objects or activities. Unlike other children with autism, these children tend to develop normally in the areas of self-help and adaptive behaviors, with the exception of social skills, which are often delayed.

## Rett's Syndrome

Also referred to as Rett's Disorder, this is a degenerative disability, meaning it gets worse with time. It begins sometime in the first two years of life and is found almost exclusively in girls. Unlike other types of autism, children with Rett's Syndrome develop normally prior to the onset of the disorder. Characteristics include loss of motor skills, hand-wringing or repetitive hand washing, and a decrease in head growth. Seizures and sleeping disorders also develop in many girls with this disorder.

## Childhood Disintegrative Disorder

This disorder, sometimes called Heller's Syndrome, is a degenerative condition in which a child may begin to develop normally, but, over a few months, will begin to lose the ability or seem to forget how to do things. It usually happens in the areas of toilet training, play skills, language, or problem-solving between ages three and four.

# When and How Is Autism Diagnosed?

Some children with autism are diagnosed by the time they are two years of age. For others, the symptoms are not recognized until they are older. Autism is, however, a medical diagnosis and requires a full examination by a qualified physician. A pediatrician, psychiatrist, or a team of medical providers may complete the medical evaluation to determine if your child meets the medical or psychological criteria for autism. While many physicians are hesitant to diagnose a child younger than two, there are benefits to an early diagnosis. The sooner your child starts receiving treatment, the better his prognosis is likely to be.

A second evaluation, given by educational personnel, will determine if the child is eligible for services such as early intervention services or speech therapy. Most states provide services to children with special needs from birth through age 21. However, each state has its own criteria for eligibility.

## How Do I Know What Services Are Available for My Child?

Once your child has been diagnosed with autism, there are laws that help determine what services she is entitled to receive. The Individuals With Disabilities Education Act (IDEA) (Public Law 101-476) outlines very specific guidelines that local school districts are required by law to adhere to when providing for the needs of children with disabilities.

For children age 3–21 with disabilities:
- **Each school district must provide a Free and Appropriate Public Education (FAPE).** This includes all

aspects of special education such as speech therapy, occupational therapy, and transportation. In addition, these services must be provided without cost to parents. Not all children with disabilities qualify for all services. Many school districts do not have programs for three-year-olds, so they may choose to contract with outside childcare providers or centers where typically developing children may be enrolled.

- **Assessments must be non-biased and non-discriminatory**. They must be conducted in your child's native language, and, most importantly, educational decisions about your child cannot be made based on a single test. In other words, a variety of assessments must be used to determine your child's eligibility for educational services. Once your child is eligible for services, an educational plan is developed and written by a team, which includes you. This team reviews and updates the Individual Education Plan (IEP) each year. Your child's IEP clearly outlines what types of service he will receive and how often he will receive the service.

- **The school's environment must be the least restrictive**. Your child must receive the service to which she is entitled in an environment that is the least restrictive. As the most recent reauthorization of IDEA makes clear, the least restrictive environment should be the general education classroom, unless there are justifications why it would not be appropriate. Many school districts elect to contract with a private preschool to provide these services.

Children from birth to age three with autism usually receive services through a state-provided comprehensive early-intervention system. Your child is assigned a service coordinator who works with you to assess your child, plan appropriate services, and develop an Individual Family Service Plan (IFSP). The IFSP is a written plan for services your child will receive, and it helps guide you as your child transitions into other programs. Children from birth to age three should receive services in their natural environment. The natural environment is the place where the child might spend time if he did not have a disability. In most cases, the natural environment is at home. However, if both parents work, the natural environment may be a school, childcare center, or a private home childcare provider.

## What Are the Common Treatments for Autism?

Because there are so many treatments for autism, it is difficult to know which one works best. Some treatments claim that certain diets or vitamins will help children with autism. In addition, addressing sensitivities to noise or smell (known as sensory integration disorders) has also allowed many children with autism to function better in a preschool setting.

The chart on the following page contains a list of the types of services that children with autism might receive.

## Services for Children with Autism

| Treatment | Definition |
| --- | --- |
| Structured Behavior Intervention | A specialist trained in applied behavior analysis (ABA) designs this plan to help your child manage his behavior. |
| Early Intervention | Services, usually home-based, which a special education teacher provides for your child. This usually describes services your child receives before he is three years old. |
| Sensory Integration Therapy | Usually an occupational therapist implements this treatment to help your child handle all the input he receives from his environment. |
| Speech/Language Therapy | A speech language pathologist works with your child to facilitate his communication and language. |
| Special Education | The special education teacher is responsible for implementing your child's Individual Education Plan (IEP) and for working with his classroom teacher to help him reach his full potential. |
| Before implementing any treatment, please consult a qualified professional such as your child's physician, speech pathologist, or special education teacher. ||

# What Do Researchers and Other Professionals Say About Children with Autism?

Despite all the available information, there is still much to learn about autism and its effects on children. However, experts do agree on two things: There is no cure for autism, and there is no plan or program that will eliminate all of the characteristics of autism. Programs that address the characteristics of autism while combining the medical and educational needs of children are most effective.

Most professionals working with children with autism agree that successful programs combine sound, structured educational programming with developmentally appropriate practices. To help your child with autism maximize his potential, it is critical for you to play an important decision-making role in planning for the education of your child. Today, scientists from such major research universities as Harvard, Vanderbilt, and Johns Hopkins are exploring what happens inside the brain of a child with autism. Using modern technology, such as Positron Emission Tomography (PET), researchers are, for the first time, able to look at the electrical energy within the brain to determine what part of the brain is responsible for certain actions and behaviors.

Increasingly, these researchers are finding evidence of a disruption or change in the brains of children with autism that is not seen in typically developing children. Other scientists are finding that in the brain of a child with autism, serotonin is broken down and used differently. In simple terms, in the brain of a typically developing child, connections are made between brain cells. Much like a computer takes in and puts out data, these connections carry information among the parts of the brain and between other parts of the body and the brain. In children with autism, these pathways, or information connections, within the brain are made differently. This could explain why children with autism often respond to sensory input so differently than their peers.

Gastroenterologists (stomach specialists) who specialize in children with autism have begun to examine closely the relationship between the brain and the child's overall physical health. They are specifically trying to determine if certain behaviors related to autism, such as hand flapping, are caused to some degree by such stomach conditions as constipation or bladder infections. Medical specialists now recognize that there are times when children with autism have a physical illness that contributes to their tantrums or violent behavior.

As a parent, it is important that you learn as much as possible about autism and that you build a support network to help you. Organizations such as Autism Society of America and Autism Speaks provide information online and help you learn about seminars and workshops that will help you work together with professionals to provide the best learning environment for your child.

## For More Information

Ball, J. 2008. *Early intervention and autism: Real life questions, real life answers.* Arlington, TX: Future Horizons

Janzen, J. E., & Therapy Skills Builders. 2000. *Autism: Facts and strategies for parents.* New York: Elsevier Science.

Jepson, B. 2007. *Changing the course of autism: A scientific approach for parents and physicians.* Bolder, Co: Sentient Publications.

Kluth, P. 2003. *You're going to love this kid!: Teaching students with autism in the inclusive classroom.* Baltimore, MD: Paul H. Brookes.

Notbohm, E. 2005. *Ten things every child with autism wishes you knew.* Arlington, TX: Future Horizons.

Sicile-Kira, C. 2004. *Autism spectrum disorders: The complete guide to understanding autism, Asperger's Syndrome, pervasive developmental disorder, and other ASDs.* New York: The Berkley Publishing Group.

## Key Terms

**Autism:** A complex developmental disability that typically appears during the first three years of life. To be diagnosed with autism, a person must demonstrate either delayed or atypical behaviors in at least one of three categories: interaction, communication, or behavior.

**Autism Spectrum Disorder (ASD):** Autism Spectrum Disorder (ASD) is a broad term which includes the classical form of autism as well as several related disabilities that share many of the same characteristics including difficulty with communication, socialization, and behavior. It is called a spectrum disorder because autism and autism-related characteristics range from very mild to very severe.

**Developmentally appropriate practices:** Activities and educational experiences that match your child's age and stage of development.

**Diagnostic and Statistical Manual of Mental Disorders, Fourth Edition-Text Revision (DSM-IV-TR):** A manual used by the American Psychological Association to diagnose and identify the characteristics of specific mental and emotional disorders.

**Echolalia:** The echoing and repetition of a phrase or word.

**Free and Appropriate Public Education (FAPE):** Special education law is clear that your child is entitled to an education that is free and appropriate for his individual needs.

**Individual Education Plan (IEP):** A personalized plan for your child, designed by a team that includes you, the child's parents. The plan outlines the educational goals and objectives for your child over a period of time (usually one school year).

**Individual Family Service Plan (IFSP):** A written plan for services your child will receive to help guide the family as your child transitions into other programs. The IFSP is written for children birth to three. Once your child turns three, an IEP is written if he still qualifies for special education services.

**Individuals With Disabilities Education Act (IDEA):** (Public Law 101-476) IDEA outlines very specific guidelines that local school districts are required by law to adhere to when providing for the needs of children with disabilities.

**Least restrictive environment:** Under the IDEA, all children who require special education services must be educated in the setting that is most appropriate to their individual needs.

**Positron Emission Tomography (PET):** Medical testing that looks at the electrical energy within the brain to determine what part of the brain is responsible for certain actions and behaviors.

**Ritualistic:** Following a set pattern or routine without variation.

**Sensory input:** Information your child receives and processes through his senses.

**Serotonin:** A hormone found in the brain. It acts as a chemical messenger that transmits signals between nerve cells. Changes in the serotonin levels in the brain can affect mood and behavior. Serotonin is also found in blood platelets and the digestive tract.

# Chapter 2

# Understanding Your Child's Behavior and Obsession with Routines

*Don't tell me my child behaves differently,
I know that already. What I want to know is do you
(his teacher) know how to help him learn?*
—*Karon, the mother of Phillip*

## How Can I Understand My Child's Unusual Behaviors?

Children with autism often behave in certain ways, such as hand-flapping or screaming out loud, that are not typically seen in other children of the same age. These unusual behaviors are sometimes called maladaptive behaviors.

Challenging behaviors may be the result of your child being:
- Frustrated or confused by a new situation or activity,
- Afraid of something,
- Overwhelmed by a panic or anxiety attack,

- Extremely angry and responds by hurting himself or a classmate,
- Very impulsive and cannot control his desire to do something,
- Attached to an inanimate object,
- Upset by the interruption of a certain ritual, or
- Stopped from doing something that is comforting to him.

## What Is Maladaptive Behavior?

By definition, maladaptive behavior is a behavior that is not common in most children or a behavior that is so severe that it interferes with learning. These behaviors can be very frustrating for you, especially when you try to help your child calm down or redirect his attention and your efforts do not work. Some maladaptive behaviors include:

- Stereotypic behavior, such as repetitive hand flapping or saying the same phrase repeatedly;
- Behaviors that are self-injurious, such as hitting or biting;
- Obsession with objects, such as collecting forks or watching the blades of a rotating ceiling fan;
- Following rituals, such as only walking on the floor instead of carpet or having to arrange food in a certain order;
- Tantrums beyond those typically seen in children; and
- Over-aggressiveness toward other children, such as hair pulling or biting.

### What Is a Stereotypic Behavior?

Stereotypic behavior is when your child repeatedly moves her body or moves an object. Some of the most common behaviors include flapping one or both hands, pulling or tapping the ears, rocking back and forth or from side to side, sniffing the air, or sucking on the upper lip. One theory about these behaviors is that children with autism may use these behaviors to "tune out" the world around them because they find certain noises over-stimulating. The stereotypic behavior gives them internal pleasure and helps them deal with the overwhelming lights, sounds, and smells in their environment. An opposite theory is that your child does these behaviors because she is under-stimulated and the stereotypic behaviors increase stimulation.

Stereotypic behavior may be a way your child calms herself. As she soothes herself by moving or rocking, her brain releases a chemical called beta-endorphin. Beta-endorphins help her body calm down and relax. Another possibility supported by research is that stereotypic behaviors may be a way children with autism communicate with adults and other children and control their environments. This is especially true when your child has limited or no language. When your child does these stereotypic behaviors, it makes you pay attention to her and then try to help her stop doing the behavior. Over time, your child may use the stereotypic behavior to get attention, which may interfere with more appropriate development of language and communication.

Stereotypic behavior is not usually harmful in itself. However, it often interferes with your child's ability to focus on what is going on around her. Occasionally, all children tune out activities they want to avoid. Even very young children will pretend not to hear when told it is time to stop playing. However, unlike typically developing children, children with autism learn that by doing a specific thing, such as rocking their body from side to side, they can temporarily tune out everything around them; it allows them to move further and further into their own world and further and further away from what is happening around them.

Over time, your child may use the stereotypic behavior to get attention, which may interfere with more appropriate development of language and communication.

## Why Would My Child Want to Hurt Herself?

Hurting oneself on purpose, or self-injurious behavior, is very different from stereotypic behavior. While your child uses stereotypic behavior to soothe herself, or when she is happy, she may hit herself repeatedly when she wants to avoid a specific activity or to get something that she wants. Self-injurious behavior is something your child does to hurt herself in an effort to get out of a situation or an environment that she finds overwhelming. Self-injurious behaviors include:

- Biting,
- Scratching (the most common places are the hand or the top of the head),
- Head banging,
- Squeezing parts of the body until they bruise, and
- Pinching parts of the body (usually the arm or hand).

Some experts believe these behaviors occur when your child is sick, such as with an ear infection. Other researchers feel that self-injury is a type of seizure over which your child has no control. Regardless of why it happens, self-injurious behaviors must be stopped immediately. Although it is rare, some self-injurious behaviors can cause permanent damage. When your child starts to injure herself, it is very important to do whatever is necessary to stop the behavior as quickly as possible. For this reason, it is a good idea to have a plan of action already in place. Perhaps you could remove your child from the immediate situation and take her to a designated place designed to help her calm down, such as a special quiet area in your child's room. This area should have soft light and a comfortable place to sit. The quiet area should never be used as a time-out or punishment area; it is available for your child to relax and escape the sensory overload she is experiencing.

## Why Is My Child Obsessed with Objects?

It is natural for your child to be attached to an object, such as a blanket or a favorite toy. This attachment helps her feel comfortable in new environments. Sometimes, when her favorite toy is nearby it helps her to cope with all the stress of dealing with other people. Most children outgrow the attachment as they grow more social and learn how to express their feelings and desires. Children with autism often develop attachments to objects or toys in a very different way than other children. For example, your child may develop an attachment to a spoon, a rock, or even the round lid of a peanut butter jar. Their attachments tend to be associated with items or objects to which their peers would not become attached.

Unlike other children, who forget about their favorite toy or blanket as soon as something new and novel gets their attention, children with autism remain obsessed with their object for hours, days, or even years. In addition, the object they are attached to often serves no functional purpose. For example, Tammy enjoys her red car because she can make it go fast on the road she built with her blocks, but as soon as she gets to preschool and sees other types of cars and trucks, she forgets about her red car and plays with the new toys. In contrast, Jill, who has autism, might be obsessed with a specific red car because she can make the left front wheel spin around repeatedly. Jill will spend a long time spinning the left front wheel over and over. When Jill gets to preschool, she will only play with that red car (the object of her obsession) and she will only spin the left front wheel. Regardless of what other toys are introduced, Jill will only play with one particular red car and only with a specific part of the red car.

## Why Does My Child Follow Rituals?

No one really knows why children with autism seem compelled to follow rituals. These rituals may involve an everyday activity, such as brushing their teeth or washing their hands. It may also be things like placing all the blocks in a certain order, getting upset when books on a shelf are not arranged by size, or if a page in a favorite book is bent. Some rituals become compulsive, which means your child will perform them repeatedly, stopping, and beginning again, if a certain step is not performed exactly the same way every time. Some researchers feel that these rituals are your child's attempt to control a world that, to him, seems out of control. Others feel it is due to the lack of a chemical in the brain called serotonin. When your child is carrying out one of these rituals, he will seem to be indifferent to the world around him and will often get very upset if this ritual or routine is interrupted for any reason.

## How Can I Recognize an Autism-Related Tantrum?

Most adults can describe what a typical two-year-old tantrum looks like. The tantrums that children with autism have are very much like those of their typically developing peers, with one exception. Typically developing children usually start to outgrow their tantrums by the time they are in preschool and/or they can be distracted by other activities, while children with autism display tantrums much more violently, much longer, and with much more energy than other children. The root cause of the tantrum may be too much environmental stimulation, such as too many sounds. These tantrums may also be triggered by things such as changes in your child's typical routine, changes in her physical environment (you rearrange toys in her room while cleaning), or the absence of usual or familiar people (your child's teacher is replaced by a substitute). Another theory is that a tantrum happens when your child goes into sensory overload.

Regardless of the cause, the tantrum is your child's attempt to convey that she is upset, unhappy, frustrated, or anxious about something. Remember, many young children with autism do not communicate their wants and needs like other children, so they may have no other way to let you know they are upset. Once your child has reached the full-blown tantrum stage, there is little, if anything, for you to do but try to keep your child from hurting herself or others. For that reason, the best way to handle tantrums is to prevent them by learning what events or actions cause them to occur. It is always good to remember that being proactive (preventing) is much easier than being reactive!

## How Can I Handle Aggressive Behavior?

Aggressive behavior is behavior that is harmful to others, such as biting, hitting, slapping, kicking, pinching, or pulling hair. Many children with autism are never aggressive toward others. However, when your child is overly tired or overly stimulated her only way to protest may be to strike what is nearest to her. Your child may sometimes resort to aggressive behavior because she has learned that it is a way to get what she wants, if only temporarily. For instance, your child may become aggressive in the hopes of receiving a certain toy or avoiding a bath.

Often, when your child is aggressive toward others, she is trying to tell you her stress level is too high. What she is really saying in the only way she knows how is, "HELP! STOP! NO!"

## How Should I Respond to My Child's Challenging Behaviors?

In general, when your child behaves in a certain way, she acts and you react. When your child hits another child or throws an object, you must react quickly.

For example, reactions to challenging behavior include:

- Praising your child when she is not behaving in a challenging manner;
- Enforcing a natural consequence for a specific action, such as not allowing your child to play with a toy for a given period after she throws that toy on the floor;
- Explaining why a behavior is not acceptable after the behavior has occurred by talking with your child; and
- Redirecting your child away from what is upsetting her, in an effort to refocus her attention on something new or novel.

For children with autism this action-reaction cycle may not stop the behavior, and may make the behavior worse. The reason a traditional action-reaction cycle is not effective for children with autism is that the strategies focus on the behavior itself and not the reason behind the behavior. When working with children with autism, it is important to look at what your child is doing (the form) and why your child is doing it (the function).

## Why Does My Child Behave in Certain Ways?

The best way to understand why your child behaves a certain way is to examine what is going on just before or just after the behavior. This is called a *functional assessment* and it helps you determine the relationship between events in your child's environment and her challenging behaviors. It involves:

- Identifying and defining the challenging behavior,
- Identifying the events and circumstances that are happening or not happening when your child is behaving in a certain way, and
- Determining the social reason behind the challenging behavior.

For example, Marissa goes outside and watches while her brothers throw a ball back and forth. When they put down the ball and go to the swings, Marissa starts to scream and hit herself. Watching her brothers throw the ball was enjoyable for Marissa. When they stopped, she was angry because she wanted to continue watching them throw the ball. In this example, Marissa's screaming was the type of behavior (the form) and her brothers stopping to throw the ball was the reason behind the behavior (the function). What Marissa was enjoying (watching her brothers play ball) was taken away from her, so she responded as a way of protesting.

The events that relate to a behavior can often help determine why the behavior occurs. These are sometimes called *setting events*—conditions that occur at the same time a challenging behavior occurs. These setting events often increase the likelihood that a challenging behavior may occur. Knowing what events or conditions may cause your child to behave in a certain way helps reduce or stop a challenging behavior before it starts. The best intervention is prevention!

The following are examples of setting events:

- A preferred caregiver's absence,
- Changes in medication,

- Sleep (too much or too little),
- Sickness (although your child may not express symptoms of feeling unwell in the same way as other children),
- Situations that are new or demanding to your child,
- An environment that is chaotic and unorganized,
- Disruptions in the regular routine of the day, such as a doctor's appointment or trip to the store,
- Changes in temperature (room temperature and weather),
- Waiting a long time for something she wants,
- Waiting too long to eat or sleep, and
- A preferred toy or item placed somewhere different.

While you may never be able to completely stop your child from behaving in a certain way, you may be able to greatly reduce her challenging behaviors by creating an environment that is proactive (preventative) rather than one that is reactive (only responds after your child misbehaves).

When planning for a positive environment, look at the following:

**The places at home or in the community where your child goes**—Look at appropriate options for your child. Sometimes, an environment or situation can be too stressful for her. There may be too many people in the setting or the activity level may be too intense. The activity may be too long, such as a trip to the grocery store.

**Keep rules and expectations simple**—Avoid too many rules or rules that are vague and abstract. Pictures that describe how you want her to act may help her learn and keep the rules in mind.

**Make consequences natural and be consistent**—Your child may become confused when there are inconsistencies in how and when things happen.

The keys to your child being successful in any setting include:

- A physical environment that is neither too stimulating nor too overwhelming for your child,
- Rules that guide behavior and are simple and concrete,
- Materials that encourage persistence and attention, and
- Routines that are easily followed and understood.

## How Do I Respond to My Child's Behavior?

What strategy you use depends on several factors. First, select a behavior that you wish to change and then decide if the

### How to Assess Your Child's Challenging Behavior

- Identify and define the challenging behavior.
- Identify the events and circumstances that are happening or not happening when your child is behaving in a certain way.
- Determine the social reason behind the challenging behavior.

reason behind the behavior (the function), such as to escape or avoid something is acceptable. For example, if your child throws a tantrum every time you ask her to stop playing and get ready for bed, you might decide that you can honor her reason (not wanting to stop playing) and teach her how to let you know that she wants more time before getting ready for bed. When your child learns to replace a negative behavior with a more acceptable behavior, such as letting you know she needs more time, you are teaching her to use a communicative replacement.

A *communicative replacement* is a form of communication or a message that your child gives you to replace the behavior. For example, you may help your child know when it is time to make a transition from play to getting ready for bed by giving her an unbreakable hourglass and telling her that when the sand runs out, it will be time to stop playing and get ready for bed. This helps your child have more control of the situation, because she can observe the hourglass and knows that there will be a set time to quit playing. This strategy may decrease her stress about the transition.

There will be behaviors you cannot allow. For example, if your child screams and hits himself every time you ask him to eat something, then you might decide that reason for his behavior is to escape eating his lunch. You cannot honor this because you know that not eating lunch could be harmful to him and might cause other problems. In this instance, you may use a strategy that would help your child control his behavior, but not allow him to escape eating. For example, you could let him listen to his favorite music while he eats or you may let him make choices about what he eats. He might prefer to eat alone with headphones on. While this does little to encourage socialization, it does disrupt the cycle of hitting himself at lunch time. In other words, the strategy you select depends on whether or not you can honor or allow the reason behind your child's behavior.

The following pages outline a few ideas and strategies to help you identify and address your child's behavior. These strategies are:
- Rejecting an Activity
- Distract and Redirect
- Waiting
- Change in Routine
- Today, I Feel…

# Rejecting an Activity

This is a strategy that you can use to teach your child how to let you know in an appropriate way when he wants to stop doing an activity, or when he would rather not complete an activity, as long as he uses an appropriate rejecting response. For example, when he has finished eating or no longer wishes to toss a ball to you.

## Materials

Hand bell, small service bell, or any other soft noisemaker (For some children loud noise is too distracting, so it is important to use a bell that makes a soft noise, not a loud ring.)

## What to Do

1. Before beginning an activity, let your child know that he may choose not to do it or stop doing it as long as he lets you know appropriately.
2. Place a bell close to where your child is working. Ring it one time as an example of an appropriate way for your child to let you know that he wants to stop doing the activity.
3. When your child rings the service bell, say, "Oh, you want to stop now."
4. Offer your child another activity and direct him to the activity. Pick up the bell and put it away. It is important that your child learn that not all activities can be stopped, which is why the bell should put away.

## Helpful Hints

- Initially, designate only one or two activities a day that your child can choose to stop and not return to finish.
- This strategy is not the same as the strategy your child might use to let you know he just needs a break.

## Distract and Redirect

Use this strategy to distract or redirect your child when he is becoming upset or when he is fixating on an object or activity. This strategy is most effective when the distraction is a preferred item or activity, and when your child is not upset, overly tired, or anxious. For example, if your child has been flapping his hands repeatedly and you want to redirect his attention to something else, or when your child has been rolling the wheel of a small car around and around and you want to help him roll the car on a flat surface.

### Materials

An object that the child likes or an activity that he enjoys

### What to Do

1. Walk up to your child and start to hum his favorite song ("Wheels on the Bus," "Itsy Bitsy Spider," or "Where Is Thumbkin?"). This will get his attention in a way that does not alarm him or upset him.
2. Point to the place or item that you wish to redirect your child toward. Look at your child, then look at the item.
3. Gently guide him toward the new object or activity. If he does not follow you, gently reach out and take his elbow or hand. Walk slowly together toward the object.
4. Sit down with your child and hand him the object.
5. Smile at him and stay a few minutes while he explores the new object.

## Waiting

Use this strategy when your child is waiting for her turn to do something or waiting in a fast food restaurant.

### Materials

An object that the child likes or an activity that he enjoys

### What to Do

1. Give your child something to do with her hands while she waits. A squishy toy or a soft squeezable object works best.
2. Play music that is soft and enjoyable so your child has something to listen to when she is waiting for a turn.
3. When you are beginning to teach this strategy, try it in a situation where there are only one or two people in line ahead of her. Waiting too long the first few times may cause her to be too anxious.
4. Later, when your child has learned to wait, she will be able to tolerate being further back in the line.
5. Verbally praise your child for waiting her turn.

### Helpful Hints

- If you play music, teach your child a few body movements that she can do while waiting.
- Try using first-then cards, which show a picture or drawing of what your child must do *first*, before *then* getting to do a preferred activity.

STRATEGY

## Change in Routine

When first using this strategy, introduce changes that might produce low or controllable levels of your child's challenging behavior, such as brief or low intensity whining or crying), rather than severe screaming and aggression.

### Materials
Child's daily schedule cards and additional cards to depict the change

### What to Do
1. Review your child's daily schedule cards with him. It is a good idea to attach the cards to a display board or wall with Velcro so that you can change them easily.
2. Talk about the schedule and what will happen next. Show him a new card that you have made and describe what the card represents. For example, "Today, we are [going to a new restaurant for lunch]. I made a picture of it for you."
3. Attach the new picture to the schedule.
4. Talk about the change. Right before it is time for the change, show the card that represents the change to your child.
5. Remind your child that this is a special activity and tell him that tomorrow the schedule will return to normal.
6. To help your child tell the difference between occasional activities and regular routine activities, make the special activity card on a different colored background such as yellow or pale orange. Be consistent. Every time there is a new occasional activity, depict it on the same color. In time, your child will understand that all activities pictured on that color card will be special or occasional in nature.

**Note:** Daily schedule cards are pictures or drawing that illustrate different daily routines, such as eating breakfast, brushing teeth, getting dressed, playing, and so on.

## Today, I Feel...

Use this enjoyable strategy to help your child learn to express how she is feeling.

### Materials

Picture cards depicting *happy, sad*, and *mad*

### What to Do

1. Make a set of feeling cards. Begin with two: happy and sad. Later, you might add other cards such as mad, surprised, and so on.
2. Talk about each card. Identify the emotion for your child. Hold up the card with the happy picture and say, "This card shows a feeling. This is happy."
3. Show your child the card that describes what you say. For example, say, "It makes me happy when you are playing." Then, hold up or point to the card showing happy.
4. Repeat the same activity using sad. Say, "It makes me sad when ____." Hold up or point to the card showing the feeling of sad.
5. Ask your child a question to see if she can point to the card that best describes how she feels. For example, "How does it make you feel when you fall down?" Then, after waiting for a response, point to the picture of sad.
6. Throughout the day, use the cards and ask your child a question. If she points to the card, say, "Thank you for telling me how you feel."
7. Use the cards until your child understands that the cards describe an emotion. It may take several days or weeks. Mount the cards where your child can see them (perhaps near your child's picture schedule) and encourage her to point to them to tell you how she is feeling.

## For More Information

Abrams, P. & L. Henriques. 2004. *The autistic spectrum: Parent's daily helper*. Berkeley, CA: Ulysses Press.

Barbera, M. & Rasmussen, T. 2007. *The verbal behavior approach: How to teach children with autism and related disorders*. London: Jessica Kingsley.

Buron, K. D. 2003. *When my autism gets too big! A relaxation book for children with autism spectrum disorders*. Shawnee Mission, KS: Autism Asperger Publishing Company.

Curtis, S. 2008. *Understanding your child's puzzling behavior: A guide for parents of children with behavioral, social, and learning challenges*. Bainbridge Island, WA: Lifespan Press.

Harris, S. L., & M.J. Weiss. 1998. *Right from the start: Behavioral Intervention for young children with autism*. Bethesda, MD: Woodbine House.

Janzen, Janice, E., & Therapy Skills Builders. 2000. *Autism: Facts and strategies for parents*. New York: Elsevier Science.

Willis, C. 2009. *Creating inclusive learning environments for young children: What to do on Monday morning*. Thousand Oaks, CA: Corwin Press.

## Key Terms

**Aggression:** Behavior that is harmful to others, such as biting, hitting, slapping, kicking, pinching, or pulling hair.

**Beta-endorphin:** A chemical in the brain that helps the body calm down and relax.

**Challenging behavior:** When your child deliberately hurts himself, injures others, and/or causes damage to his environment.

**Communicative replacement:** A form of communication or a message that your child gives to you that replaces the behavior.

**Compulsive:** Behaviors your child performs repeatedly that will be stopped and begun again if a certain step is not performed exactly the same way every time.

**Cue:** A hint that is a word, gesture, or phrase.

**Form:** The way your child behaves. Examples of forms of behavior are hitting, biting, and so on.

**Function:** The reason why something happens. The function of a behavior is the reason behind the behavior.

**Functional assessment**: An evaluation designed to determine the relationship between events in your child's environment and the occurrence of challenging behaviors.

**Maladaptive behavior:** A behavior that is not common in most children or one that is so severe that it interferes with learning.

**Natural consequence**: The logical result of an action.

**Obsession:** A strong inclination toward something to the point of excluding everything else, such as collecting forks or watching the blades of a rotating ceiling fan.

**Proactive**: A procedure or action that happens before a problem occurs and is designed to prevent the problem or behavior from occurring.

**Ritual:** A pattern or way of doing something that is not logical, such as only walking on the floor instead of carpet or having to arrange food in a certain order before it can be eaten.

**Self-injurious behavior:** Something your child does to hurt herself, such as hitting or biting herself, in an effort to get out of a situation or an environment that is overwhelming.

**Setting event:** Conditions that occur at the same time a challenging behavior occurs.

**Stereotypic behavior:** A behavior that is carried out repeatedly and involves either your child's moving his body or moving an object, such as repetitive hand flapping or saying the same phrase repeatedly.

**Tantrum:** Anger beyond what is normally seen in children, such as falling to the floor and screaming or throwing their bodies on the ground.

# Chapter 3

# Using Signs, Symbols, and Language to Help Your Child Communicate

*If a child has no reason to communicate,*
*why should he even try?*
—*Helen, the mother of Nathan*

## What Exactly Is Communication?

Communication is an interaction between two or more people where information is exchanged, when one person sends a message to another person. Communication has three essential aspects (described in the chart on the following page): form, function, and content.

**Essential Aspects of Communication**

| Communication | Definition | Example |
| --- | --- | --- |
| Form | A way to communicate | Crying, talking, gestures, using sign language, pointing to picture cards |
| Function | A reason to communicate | Being hungry, wanting something, needing something or someone, needing attention |
| Content | Purpose of communication | Your child needs experiences and opportunities to explore so he will have something to communicate about. |

# How Does My Child Communicate Differently Than Other Children?

Most children with autism have a smaller vocabulary and difficulty understanding and using language in social settings. Language disorders are often typical of children with autism. In fact, it may be the most noticed characteristic. A language disorder is defined as a deficit in using words or vocabulary. It can also involve how a child understands language and uses it in social settings. For children with autism, a pragmatic language delay is often seen. Pragmatic language involves using language in a social setting. For example, knowing what is appropriate to say, when to say it, and the general give-and-take nature of friendly conversations. Because autism is a spectrum ranging from severe to very mild, children with autism will have communication abilities that range from not talking at all (nonverbal) to being able to communicate very well. Often, children with autism who talk will appear to use words and speech in a way that is not meaningful (non-functional).

# What Is Communication That Is Not Meaningful?

Communication that is not meaningful (non-functional) is speech that is understood and spoken clearly but has no relevance to the interaction that is taking place. For example, four-year-old Evan knows how to talk and does so frequently, but when you ask him to go outside, he simply says, "Bottom of the ninth and the bases are loaded." Evan is communicating. In fact, he *is* answering the question. Unfortunately, he is answering it in a non-functional manner. However, sometimes what sounds like non-functional communication can, with careful observation, be the child's way of answering in a way that makes sense to him. In other words, there are times when non-functional communication does having meaning for the child. Once you understand that meaning, the communication becomes meaningful. What Evan really means is, "Going outside is very stressful."

# How Can Non-Functional Communication Be Functional?

To answer this question, let's examine how Larry answers questions. He is five, knows about colors, and can name and describe each of them. However, when asked, "Larry, what is your favorite color?" he replies, "Lemon yellow." On the other hand, when asked, "Would you like to go to the store?" he replies "Crimson red." It appears that he is answering the first question appropriately or functionally, while his answer to the second question is non-functional and not appropriate.

Larry's family has been observing his communication for some time and has determined that every time Larry responds with "crimson red" it is Larry's way of saying "No!" They have also observed that when Larry means "yes," he answers with "sunset orange." His family, through observation and experience, has learned to interpret the meaning behind Larry's non-functional communication. But it does not mean that Larry's family should stop encouraging him to answer "yes" or "no." It means that, while he is learning to answer "yes" and "no," his family knows how to interpret how Larry expresses his wishes.

Children who have difficulties with meaningful (functional) communication may use echolalia when responding to questions. It can be very frustrating when everything you say is repeated back to you.

# What Exactly Is Echolalia?

*Echolalia* is the echoing and repetition of a phrase or word. Echolalia can be an instant response—meaning that your child will repeat a phrase immediately after he hears it. For example, you say, "Let's go wash the car" and your child immediately repeats, "Let's go wash the car." Your child may repeat the phrase multiple times. Often, echolalia cannot be controlled or stopped on command. There are times when your child may not even be aware he is doing anything out of the ordinary.

Sometimes, children use echolalia as a way to intentionally communicate. The repeated phrase has meaning to your child, and he attempts to use the phrase in conversation. For example, when you ask Bailey about her day at school, Bailey might respond with the phrase "time for small group," as a way to communicate that she went to group time at school.

Delayed echolalia occurs hours, days, or weeks after it is first heard. This type of echolalia is unpredictable and may happen because your child hears a phrase he likes. For example, Dusty heard the expression, "Beam me up, Scotty!" from the television series *Star Trek*. He used the expression over and over all day long, much to the frustration of his family. However, when they observed the context or the situations in which he used it most often, they found it was when he was frustrated or when a new activity had been introduced. In his own way, Dusty was using the phrase, "Beam me up, Scotty!" to express his anxiety over the new task. While the expression in itself made no sense to others, for Dusty, it had meaning.

Paula Kluth, in her book *You're Going to Love This Kid*, suggests several ways to respond to echolalia. First, she suggests that you reassure your child. You might say, "I think you are trying to tell me ____." or "I am sorry. I don't understand. Are you trying to tell me ____?" Your response is an attempt to show your child that you are listening and encourages your child to keep trying to articulate his wishes.

Kluth's second strategy is called "going to the movies," which means that when your child repeats a phrase from a movie or television show, you try to determine if your child is using that phrase to communicate a message. Once you have figured out what the phrase means to your child, a key for others to follow can easily be made. For example, Dusty uses the phrase, "Beam me up, Scotty!" when he is frightened because to him, it means, "I'm scared and don't understand what to do next."

Another technique for handling echolalia is to use it to your benefit. For example, ask your child, "Do you want a cookie?" and your child replies, "Do you want a cookie?" You then say what you want your child to say, "Yes, I want a cookie." This allows you to help your child understand the relationship between what your child says and what is intended.

Finally, the work of Gail Gillingham has suggested that some children with echolalia respond better when you talk in a whisper. The idea is that your child has to listen intently to hear you talk, so he does not respond with echolalia.

# Why Does My Child Have So Much Trouble Communicating?

Effective communication is more than just sending and receiving messages. It requires that one person, either the sender or the receiver of the message, interact with the other person. Actually, for the interaction to be successful, the other person must reciprocate in some way. In initiating an exchange of a message or information, the sender must be willing to approach the person she will be communicating with. Although your child may be able to answer a direct question or make a statement about what he wants, starting a conversation is especially difficult. In fact, your child is more likely to initiate a communication when he wants or needs something. It is less likely he will initiate communication simply for the sake of a social interaction.

Communication is divided into expressive and receptive. Expressive communication has to do with how your child uses communication to express himself. Receptive communication is how your child receives messages or information from others. Speech-language pathologists and other experts in the field of communication have always believed that children can receive messages much earlier than they can generate them—receptive language develops before expressive language.

Speech-language pathologists are excellent resources for helping you determine not only how and why your child communicates, but what can be done to enhance his communication. For your child to communicate effectively, he must be able to communicate on purpose. This is called intentional communication.

> Speech-language pathologists are excellent resources for helping you determine not only how and why your child communicates, but what can be done to enhance his communication. For your child to communicate effectively, he must be able to communicate on purpose. This is called intentional communication.

# What Is Intentional Communication?

Intentional communication is communication that happens for a reason. It is purposeful. When your child randomly points toward a toy without really indicating that he wants to hold it, he is using unintentional communication. However, if you hold the toy out for him and he reaches for it, he will soon learn that by pointing to an object you will give it to him.

This example illustrates the importance of responding to your child's attempts to communicate, whether or not the attempt is intentional. This is especially true of children with autism, who often do not attempt to communicate intentionally.

# How Do I Start Helping My Child Communicate?

The best place to start is by observing your child until you can determine what methods or actions he uses to communicate and under what conditions he is most likely to communicate.

In general terms, your child will communicate when:
- He is able to pay attention to what is being said,
- He is able to understand what is said by others,
- He has experienced people responding to his attempts at communication, and
- He has a reason to communicate.

It is also important to find out what motivates your child. Look for reasons why he might or might not communicate. Recognize that he may not communicate in the same way as his peers. For example, if Kirby throws his food when you place it in front of him, he may be communicating that he does not want to eat. In this case, it would be helpful for you and his speech pathologist to work together to figure out an alternative way for him to communicate that he is not hungry. You will need to determine his stage of communication. Trying to force your child to communicate before he is ready only frustrates him and may also delay his progress.

## What Are the Stages of Communication?

The various stages of communication have been given a variety of names and defined in many different ways. This book describes the stages that preschool children might experience, including:

- "It's all about me"—Egocentric Stage,
- "I want it"—Requesting Stage,
- Actions and reactions—Emerging Communication Stage, and
- Two-way street—Reciprocal Communication Stage.

If you want more information, consult a speech pathologist about the traditional developmental stages of communication.

### Egocentric Stage

The "It's All About Me" (egocentric) stage usually occurs when children are around two years old. Because children with autism may be delayed in their overall development, it is not uncommon for your child to communicate in this stage for one or more years after age two.

If your child is in the egocentric stage he might:

- Reach his hands out to indicate "I want,"
- Scream or cry when he does not get something he wants,

- Smile or laugh when someone looks at him,
- Be very shy around strangers,
- Not interact with other children, but interact with adults who are familiar to him, or
- Experiment with how language sounds and say phrases repeatedly.

## Requesting Stage

The "I want it" (requesting) stage occurs as your child learns cause and effect. He begins to understand that what he says or does has an effect on people or on his environment. During this stage, your child starts to see communication as a means to get what he wants.

If your child is in the requesting stage he might:
- Grab your hand and pull you toward something he wants,
- Say a few basic words,
- Move his body when you are interacting with him to communicate "I want more,"

more

- Begin to sign the word "more" by putting his hands together, or
- Approximate words or attempt a few new words.

## Emerging Communication Stage

Your child is in the emerging communication stage when she starts to understand that she can repeat the same action, gesture, or word and get the same result. In this stage, she will put two words together and seem to enjoy repeating what she just heard. These communication interactions with your child are much longer and more sustained than in the previous stages.

If your child is in the emerging communication stage she might:

- Take turns,
- Understand the names of those familiar to her,
- Repeat what she just heard,
- Use gestures more consistently, such as shaking her head "no,"
- Answer simple questions,
- Ask for something or request that you continue something, or
- Use words or signs in a more meaningful way.

## Reciprocal Communication Stage

The "Two-Way Street" (reciprocal communication) stage is characterized by direct communication with a partner. Often, children in this stage are more prone to communicate with an adult than with a peer. While children with autism continue to have difficulty initiating or beginning conversations with peers, children with autism may participate in a conversation if they have a strong need or a motivation to get something from another child.

Children with autism rarely initiate spontaneous communication. They still need conversations to be very concrete and literal. Children in this stage of communication may have difficulty with social cues, new social situations, and understanding the abstracts of language, such as jokes. They also have difficulty understanding when someone is kidding them or making light of something.

If your child is in the reciprocal communication stage he might:

- Intentionally use words to greet someone, ask for something, protest something, ask questions, and tell someone about something;
- Express ideas and feelings that are relevant to him;
- Have short conversations (although he will always be more easily distracted than his peers);

- Repeat something, if he thinks the listener does not understand; or
- Start to use longer sentences with more descriptive words.

# How Do I Set Appropriate Goals for Communication?

It is difficult to know which goals to set when your child is learning to communicate. It is equally challenging to know what to expect from your child. While each child is unique and will communicate in his own way, there are several general suggestions to think about when setting communication goals.

1. In order to communicate effectively, your child must have a reliable form or way to communicate. It is important to help your child use a form that will help him interact with others.
2. The ultimate goal for any child is to learn to communicate because it is meaningful to him. You want your child to learn to do more than just tell you what he wants and needs; you want him to learn to use communication as a form of self-expression.
3. Communication should be meaningful. Help your child learn to communicate a way to connect his world with that of his peers.

The ultimate goal for any child is to learn to communicate because it is meaningful to him. You want your child to learn to do more than just tell you what he wants and needs; you want him to learn to use communication as a form of self-expression.

In addition to the general guidelines above, the communication goals found in the chart below are based on the child's stage of communication.

## Communication Goals

| Stage of Communication | Goals |
| --- | --- |
| Egocentric Stage | ■ "Nothing is free"—Require your child to show you what he wants by pointing, gesturing, or using sign language.<br>■ Play simple games that involve taking turns, such as rolling a ball back and forth. Verbalize what you are doing. Say, "It is my turn" and point to yourself, then say, "It is your turn" and point to your child.<br>■ Consistently respond to every communication attempt, even if it is unintentional.<br>■ Describe what the child is doing. |
| Requesting Stage | ■ Play a game or start an activity. Then, stop playing and try to get your child to request "more," either by moving his body or looking at you.<br>■ When your child pulls you toward something or points to a desired object, respond. Then, say aloud what he wanted and say the name of the object.<br>■ Describe everything your child does using simple sentences.<br>■ Children with autism often respond poorly to continuous talk. They are under-responsive to verbal stimuli. Provide a model. Say it from your child's point of view. Wait expectantly, and show him ways to let you know what he needs such as pointing, gesturing, or nodding. |

## Communication Goals *(cont'd.)*

| Stage of Communication | Goals |
|---|---|
| Emerging Stage | <ul><li>Continue to play games that involve taking turns, but encourage your child to play with other children whenever possible.</li><li>Provide an exact model of what you want your child to say and do.</li><li>Respond to any situations when your child initiates a communication interaction.</li><li>Build on your child's expanding vocabulary by giving him experiences that will help him develop new words.</li><li>If your child is using pictures to communicate, encourage him to use words, too.</li></ul> |
| Reciprocal Stage | <ul><li>Set up situations that encourage conversation.</li><li>Throughout all stages, the environment plays a major role in helping your child interact.</li><li>Play games during which you practice the rules of conversation, such as starting, stopping, and waiting for a turn.</li><li>Help your child use communication for more than just simple requests. Talk about communicating feelings or opinions.</li><li>Ask other children, such as his siblings or cousins, to be peer buddies and talk him.</li></ul> |

# Should I Stop Trying to Make My Child Talk and Use an Alternative Form of Communication Instead?

While learning to talk is always important, it may not be possible for all children. What is most important is that children communicate with purpose. When your child is not using words or word-like noises to request items, or does not comment about things or respond to questions, it is time to consider using an alternative way to communicate. This does not necessarily mean she will never learn to speak. It may mean that she needs a bridge or a way to help her as she learns to speak.

An alternative communication system is generally a method of communication that does not involve speech. Some children who remain nonverbal may ultimately use devices that speak for them. However, for most nonverbal preschool children, a more functional system will include either sign language or pictures. Even if your child is starting to use speech, she can use sign language and/or pictures to supplement her communication and facilitate comprehension and organization. These tools can also reduce the frustration she feels when she is unable to let people in her world know what she wants. Remember, children with autism are usually strong visual learners and visual communication systems allow them to understand their environment and express what they are feeling.

Numerous studies have shown using alternative communication aides, like visual symbols, will not keep your child from talking. Rather, these studies show that communication supports help children, and enhance the ability of children who do develop spoken language to do so more effectively. Work with your child's teacher and other professionals to understand and support the communication system that is most beneficial to your child.

## When and How Is the Best Way to Use Sign Language?

Sign language can help your child communicate with the people in his world. Although some children do not have the motor skills to make signs or make up their own rather than use standard signs, sign language can be a valuable tool that you can use to help your child learn to communicate. If you have decided to use basic signs with him, it is always a good idea to make a list of the signs as he learns them, so others in his world will be able to communicate with him. Learning signs together can become a game that the whole family can enjoy.

Decide which signs to teach first, keeping in mind the signs might help your child most. Three signs—*want*, *more*, and *all done* (finished) represent things that your child might use frequently throughout the day. (For more information about teaching sign language see page 69.) These three signs are a starting place because they communicate basic things for your child, and can be used in a variety of everyday situations. The chart on the following page includes pictures of some of the most commonly used signs.

## Commonly Used Signs

| Word | Sign | Word | Sign |
|------|------|------|------|
| eat | | drink | |
| bathroom | | inside | |
| outside | | more | |
| play | | thank you | |

Remember, just because your child begins to use signs to communicate does not necessarily mean he will always use signs. But whether sign language is a bridge to using more traditional forms of communication or a method that the child will use throughout his life, it will enable him to let others know what he wants and needs.

# How Can My Child Use Pictures to Communicate?

 Pictures are more universal than sign language. Anyone can understand if your child points to a picture of a toy that means he would like to play with the toy. Handing a picture to you is one way that your child can interact with you. With pictures, your child can indicate a choice, a preference, or answer a question.

The most widely recognized formal system of communication is the Picture Exchange System (PECS), developed by Andy Bondy and Lori Frost. Information about PECS can be found on www.pyramidproducts.com. In the PECS system, your child presents pictures to you or another person or selects pictures from a board or portable notebook. The pictures are inexpensive and portable, allowing your child to use them in a variety of different situations. While pictures are an excellent teaching tool for your child, using the official PECS system requires special training, as there is a very specific method to presenting each sequence of pictures.

Pictures are great teaching tools, are practical and easy to use, and also provide the opportunity for your child to use the same set of pictures in different settings—at home, at school, or in his community. When using a picture communication system you will want to use the following guidelines:

- Help your child learn how to use the pictures. Post picture schedules for the day and refer to them often throughout the day. Use them to explain the sequence of an activity.

Whenever you introduce a new word, hold up the corresponding picture.

■ The ultimate goal in using a picture system is to teach your child to initiate communication. Once your child is adept at using pictures, encourage him to use them to start a communication interaction.

■ Build a list of commonly used pictures and practice with your child. You might ask him to point to the picture that shows what he wants. Please keep in mind that because children with autism have difficulty with abstract concepts, it may take lots of practice before your child understands that the pictures represent an object or an activity.

■ Expand the picture list and ask questions that require your child to answer you by pointing to a picture.

■ As your child becomes more comfortable with using the picture communication system, expand the pictures to include action pictures and pictures that he can use to tell you what and how he is feeling.

### How to Use a Picture System

■ Help your child learn how to use the pictures.

■ Encourage your child to use the pictures to start a communication interaction.

■ Build a list of commonly used pictures and practice with your child.

■ Send pictures to school and encourage your child's teacher to use them.

■ Expand the picture list and ask questions that require your child to answer you by pointing to a picture.

■ Expand the pictures to include action pictures and pictures that your child can use to tell you what and how he is feeling.

# What About Electronic Communication Devices?

While there are a few electronic communication devices simple enough for a young child to learn to use, these devices, which are designed to provide a source of communication, specifically speech, are often too expensive or too complex for a young child to use. However, if an electronic device is used, there are guidelines to consider:

- Be sure that the voice recorded on the device is a child's voice, not the voice of an adult.
- Contact the manufacturer of the device. Most manufacturers are happy to provide a free demonstration or, at the very least, provide materials about how the device works.
- Remember that the device belongs to your child. It is his voice and is not a toy to be used by other children.
- Find out what size batteries the device uses and keep plenty on hand.

Single message switches, such as the Big-Mack Jellybean Switch by AbleNet, are sometimes used to help children as they begin to communicate. It uses a button-type switch on which a single message has been recorded. You teach your child to push the button for a specific message. Many parents start by using a single button or single message switch to help their child signal when he needs to go to the bathroom. A picture of a bathroom or a toilet can easily be taped or attached to the switch. Whenever your child needs to go to the bathroom, he just walks up to the switch and pushes the button. One advantage of this device is that it is easy to change the message and the device is easy to operate.

Communication is a lifelong learning skill that facilitates social relationships and helps your child relate to his environment. Regardless of how much or how little your child communicates, it is important that you understand the following:

- How to encourage interactions,
- How he communicates best,
- Why he communicates, and
- How to model language.

---

The following pages outline a few ideas and strategies to help you teach your child how to communicate. These strategies are:

- A Reason to Communicate!
- Three Basic Signs
- What Is It? Using Pictures to Identify Objects
- Sing to Me: Using Music to Communicate
- Picture This! Communication Notebooks
- Learning to Communicate "Yes" and "No!"

## A Reason to Communicate!

This activity forces your child to request, protest, and/or comment on what is going on. The more effectively you can create these opportunities, the greater the likelihood that your child's communication will become intentional.

### Materials

A toy or object that your child likes

### What to Do

1. Place an object slightly out of your child's reach. Wait, and when your child begins to make noises or move toward the object, pretend that you do not know what he wants. If your child makes any attempt to request the item (gesture, sign, and so on), hand it to him and say, "Oh, you wanted the ____."

2. Another way to encourage your child to request an object is to place an object that he likes in a container that he cannot open so he has to gesture, sign, or indicate what he wants you to do.

3. To further encourage your child to tell you what he wants, pretend you do not know, and see if he will persist in trying to tell you or show you what he wants.

4. If your child is in a patient mood, hand him the wrong object and look at him as if you do not know what he wants. Do not frustrate him. Try to encourage the rule that "Nothing is free!" He must ask, gesture, or sign to get what he wants.

5. Deliberately say or do something in your daily routine that is wrong. Sometimes children with autism will feel a compulsion to correct your mistake. This can lead to a more functional use of language.

## Three Basic Signs

When your child is ready, teach her three basic signs: *want*, *more*, and *all done*. Let your child's teacher and other professionals know which signs your child is learning so that they also use the same signs.

**Materials**
None

**What to Do**
1. Practice the signs so you can make them correctly.

**Three Basic Signs**

| Want | More | All done (finished) |
|------|------|---------------------|

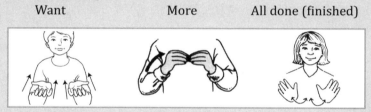

2. Once you are confident that you know the three basic signs, begin to use them with your child.
3. Always say the word as you sign it.
4. Don't force your child to use the signs. Simply model each sign as you use it.
5. Praise your child for any attempt to imitate the sign.
6. After your child is familiar with the three basic signs, encourage her to use them to let you know when she wants more and when she is finished.

**Helpful Hints**
- Make learning the signs a game everyone can play.
- Encourage close friends and grandparents to use the signs with the child.

## What Is It? Using Pictures to Identify Objects

Teach your child to use pictures to identify objects because even if your child knows certain vocabulary words, he may not understand how to use them to communicate.

### Materials

10 pictures that represent a specific item or activity (avoid pictures with a lot of detail—black-and-white line drawings usually work best); and 10 objects that match each picture

### What to Do

1. Select 10 pictures that you want to use with your child. Make sure the pictures clearly represent one specific item or activity.
2. Select pictures that are useful for your child. Start with pictures and real objects, such as a cup, a ball, a book, and a paintbrush, and pictures of these objects.
3. Pick up the object and the picture. Hand the object to your child. If he does not take it, try to direct his attention to the object. To help your child make the transition from pictures to objects, put the objects in small resealable sandwich bags for easy use and handling. It is easier for a child to understand that a picture is a representation of a real object when he sees the picture and the object together.
4. Point to the picture and say the word.
5. Start with one or two pictures and build up to 10.
6. Remember that the purpose is to help your child make the connection between the picture and the object.

## Sing to Me: Using Music to Communicate

Use familiar songs and rhymes to help your child communicate. She may sing when she might not be as open to a conversation.

**Materials**
None

**What to Do**

1. Choose simple songs with tunes the child recognizes. Songs with repeating words often work best. Don't be concerned if you can't sing well; it's the interaction that children find enjoyable.
2. Sing about activities or things that the child enjoys. Stress key words, concepts, or vocabulary.
3. Use the child's name whenever possible.
4. Consider the following examples.

**New Foods** (*A song to encourage eating*)
(Tune: "Mary Had a Little Lamb")
*Mark is eating peas today, peas today, peas today,*
*Mark is eating peas today, I am so glad.*

Or

____ (child's name) *is trying* ____ (name of new food) *today,* ____ (name of new food) *today,* ____ (name of new food) *today,*
____ (child's name) *is trying* ____ (name of new food) *today, I am so glad.*

*(cont'd. on next page)*

**Play with Me!** (a *song to encourage playing together*)
(Tune: "Twinkle, Twinkle, Little Star")
*Won't you come and play with me?*
*We'll have fun, just wait and see.*
*First it's your turn, then it's mine.*
*We'll be friends all the time.*
*Won't you come and play with me?*
*We'll have fun, just wait and see.*

**An Action Song** (*a song to describe an action*)
(Tune: "Row, Row, Row Your Boat")
*Terrance has a blue car.*
*It's his favorite toy.*
*He will roll it up and down.*
*Terrance has a blue car.*

5. Once your child learns the song, leave out words and wait expectantly for the child to fill them in. She may use a word picture, sign, or gesture to fill in the missing part of the song.

**Helpful Hints**
- Encourage other children at home to help you write songs.
- Sing in a pleasant tone, keeping in mind that loud noises can overwhelm your child.

## Picture This! Communication Notebooks

Communication notebooks are great tools to use to encourage your child to express his feelings. Communication notebooks also make great conversation starters.

### Materials

Photo album or individual pocket pages with accompanying pictures

### What to Do

1. Photo albums with individual pockets for pictures make great holders for your child's pictures. Wallets with fold-out plastic photo holders can also be used to make great picture stories.
2. To begin, take a single experience that your child has had and see if he will point to some pictures that tell you about what he saw, felt, or did. You can prompt your child by providing hints and picture cues.
3. Write a sentence to go with each page in the book.
4. Your child can also use communication books to help him express his emotions.
5. Encourage your child to carry his communication book with him and refer to it whenever possible.

### Helpful Hints

■ Encourage your child's teachers to make communication books at school and send them home. Knowing what the child enjoys at home can be very helpful to the teacher who is looking for conversation starters.
■ Use communication notebooks as problem solvers to help the child figure out how to do something.

## Learning to Communicate "Yes" and "No!"

The sooner your child can let you know what she wants, the less likely she may be to have a tantrum because she feels no one understands her needs.

**Materials**

None

**What to Do**

1. Determine the most likely manner in which your child can be prompted to use the concept of yes/no. These might include: sign for yes/no, nodding or shaking the head, or saying it verbally.

   Yes                    No

2. Play a game where you ask the child yes/no questions. Begin with objects. For example, hold up a book and say, "Is this a book?"
3. Pause, and give your child time to answer.
4. As your child learns to respond, ask her questions about people, such as, "Are you a girl?" or "Is this your daddy?"
5. Expand the activity to include questions about color, size, shape, and actions.
6. As your child begins to use yes/no more consistently, ask her questions about herself, such as, "Is your shirt red?" or "Do you want to go to the park?"

## For More Information

Gillingham, G. 2000. *Autism, a new understanding*. Edmonton, Alberta, Canada: Tacit Publishing, Inc.

Pepper, J. & Weitzman, E. 2004. *It takes two to talk.* Toronto: The Hanen Centre.

Small, M. & L. Kontente. 2003. *Everyday solutions: A practical guide for families of children with autism spectrum disorders*. Shawnee Mission, KS: Autism Asperger Publishing Company.

Sussman, F. 2006 *Talkability: People skills for verbal children on the autism spectrum: A guide for parents.* Toronto: The Hanen Centre.

## Key Terms

**Alternative communication system:** A method of communication that does not involve speech.

**Communication:** An interaction between two or more people where information is exchanged.

**Echolalia:** The echoing and repetition of a phrase or word.

**Electronic communication device:** Sometimes called an augmentative communication device; a mechanical device that is designed to talk for your child when it is activated either by a switch or by pressing a button.

**Expressive communication:** How your child communicates to others.

**Intentional communication**: Communication that is on purpose or deliberate.

**Language disorder:** A deficit in using words or vocabulary. It can also involve how your child understands language and uses it in social settings.

**Non-functional communication:** Communication that lacks meaning or purpose.

**Pragmatic language:** Involves using language in a social setting. For example, knowing what is appropriate to say, when to say it, and the general give-and-take nature of a friendly conversation.

**Receptive communication:** How your child receives messages or information from others.

# Chapter 4

# Lights! Camera! Action! Sensory Integration and Autism

*We don't even try to take Kristen to the store anymore.*
*It's just not worth the hassle.*
*—Rita, the mother of Kristen*

## What Is Sensory Integration?

Sensory Integration (SI) is a process that occurs in the brain. It allows us to take in information through our senses, organize it, and respond accordingly to the environment. It is also the process that allows us to filter out any unneeded sensory information. For example, when you walk into a noisy restaurant, it is sensory integration that gives you the ability to filter out the surrounding noise so that you can enjoy your lunch or chat with a friend. In addition to the obvious senses: sight, hearing, touch, taste, and smell, there are two "hidden" senses that are just as important: *vestibular* and *proprioceptive*.

# What Are the Hidden Senses?

Both the vestibular sense and the proprioceptive sense help your child integrate all the information he receives from the environment.

The vestibular sense provides information through the inner ear about balance, movement, and gravity. In other words, it is the vestibular sense that lets your child know how to position his head and body.

The vestibular sense affects:
- Your child's sense of balance or equilibrium,
- The way your child's eyes and hands work together (eye-hand coordination),
- Your child's ability to move both sides of his body together, and
- The way your child moves his head.

The proprioceptive system receives information from joints, muscles, and ligaments. It is this sense that lets your child know where the parts of his body are and what they are doing. For example, this system might tell your child how far it is for him to reach to pick up a toy and how much pressure is comfortable or uncomfortable to parts of his body.

These two senses work together to help regulate the nervous system and allow your child to move with purpose. When your child cannot regulate the information he receives from his senses, he is often diagnosed with a Sensory Integration Disorder.

# What Is a Sensory Integration Disorder?

Almost 50 years ago, an occupational therapist named Jean Ayres used the term Sensory Integration Dysfunction (SI Dysfunction) to describe a child who is unable to analyze and respond appropriately to the information he receives from his senses. A child with sensory integration dysfunction has problems adapting to the everyday sensations that others take for granted. Today, the terms Sensory Integration Dysfunction, Sensory Integration Disorder, and Sensory Modulation Disorder are used interchangeably. Regardless of which term is used, many experts believe that a sensory integration problem is the root cause of many of the behaviors commonly seen in children with autism.

# Do You Mean That My Child Sees or Hears Differently?

Children with autism can hear and see just like other children. What many are unable to do, however, is to take the information that they see, hear, taste, feel, or touch and translate it into a meaningful response. In other words, what may seem like normal lighting to you might seem like megawatt spotlights to your child. The normal chatter heard in a room can feel unbearably loud to your child. Your child may be unable to regulate or modulate the input they receive through their senses. Because such information is sometimes so overpowering, they will have problems learning and interacting in their environments.

Most children enjoy dancing to a favorite tune, jumping up and down, touching new things, using their hands to make a mountain from clay, or painting with their fingers. Children like to listen to a story, play in the dirt or sandbox, and smell a fresh flower with delight. However, if your child has a sensory integration disorder, these activities can be frightening, confusing, and overwhelming.

# How Will I Know If My Child Has a Sensory Integration Disorder?

You will recognize if your child has a sensory integration disorder through observation, through information you receive from others, and by educating yourself about ways to recognize it. A few of the most common red flags that might indicate that your child has a sensory integration disorder include unusual responses to touch, adverse responses to moving and being moved, a lack of tolerance for noise and light, and an unwillingness to taste or try new foods.

The following are a few examples of how a child with sensory integration disorder might respond to everyday situations:

*Scott walks into the bathroom and looks around. He immediately goes to the sink and turns on the faucet. He watches as the water comes out. He places his hands in the water. He fails to notice anything except the running water. In fact, he may become so fascinated by the water he ignores everything around him.*

*It is time to get ready for lunch and you have called Maria by name several times. Instead of responding or coming into the kitchen, Maria continues to stare at the rotating blades of the ceiling fan as they whirl around on her bedroom ceiling. She does not seem to hear you call her name.*

*Mi-Ling does not enjoy sitting down, and she will not sit still while you read to her. She stands up and begins to spin around and around.*

These are all examples of how a child with autism who has a sensory integration disorder might respond. Some children, like the ones in the examples above, are over-sensitive (*hypersensitive*) to sensory stimulation, and other children with autism are actually under-sensitive (*hyposensitive*). These children seem to be in another sphere where they can't see, hear, feel, or touch anything at all. Children who are under-sensitive to sensory information are at great risk for getting hurt. Because they don't often respond normally to sound, they may walk in front of a car. A child who is under-sensitive might pick up a hot object or fall down a flight of stairs without ever letting you know he feels pain.

## How Do I Know If My Child Is Over-Sensitive or Under-Sensitive?

The chart below outlines how your child might respond to different situations. However, your child's occupational therapist is your best resource for information about sensory integration disorder.

## Sense Responses

| Sense | Over-Sensitive | Under-Sensitive |
|-------|----------------|-----------------|
| Vision (sight) | ■ Covers his eyes when the lights are too bright<br>■ Overwhelmed by too many colors and items in the classroom<br>■ Rubs his eyes or squints his eyes frequently | ■ Does not respond to light<br>■ Holds items close to her face as if she can't see them<br>■ Stares at flickering fluorescent lights |
| Sound | ■ Covers his ears<br>■ Responds to sounds other children ignore<br>■ Will act as if he can't hear when you call his name, but then responds when a child drops a toy<br>■ Yells with fingers in ears | ■ Speaks loudly<br>■ Turns the volume up on the TV or computer<br>■ Sings loudly<br>■ Always plays with toys that make loud noises |
| Smell | ■ Holds her nose at common odors<br>■ Sniffs the air or sniffs other people | ■ Ignores bad odors<br>■ May sniff people or toys |
| Touch (tactile) | ■ Gets upset when someone touches him<br>■ Very sensitive to textures and materials | ■ Bumps into people<br>■ Chews on items frequently<br>■ Unaware of temperature changes |

**Sense Responses** *(cont'd.)*

| Sense | Over-Sensitive | Under-Sensitive |
|---|---|---|
| | ■ Opposed to getting dirty or touching certain toys<br>■ Scratches at his skin or startles when something touches him | ■ Seemingly unable to tell when he is in pain or hurt<br>■ Does not cry when he falls down |
| Taste | ■ Gags when she eats<br>■ Only eats food of a certain texture<br>■ Sensitive to hot or cold foods | ■ Wants only spicy food<br>■ Adds a lot of pepper or salt to her food<br>■ Licks objects or toys |
| Movement | ■ Does not like to move, dance, climb, or hop<br>■ Sways<br>■ Seems to walk "off-balance" | ■ Does not get dizzy when he whirls or turns around<br>■ Loves to move fast<br>■ In constant motion<br>■ Rocks back and forth<br>■ Moves his body all the time |

# What Can I Do to Help My Child?

Your child may respond well to items that help him to calm down so that he can handle the input he receives through his senses. These objects include: things to chew on (chewies), toys that vibrate, weighted vests, soft things to squeeze, beanbag chairs or therapy balls to sit on, and stretchy material such as latex that he can use to make a body cocoon.

The most common examples are:

**Chewies:** If your child has issues relating to touch, chewing on something soft can be very relaxing. Chewies can be purchased from companies that specialize in sensory integration materials.

**Vibrating toys:** Vibration can be very calming to the proprioceptive system. Examples of vibrating items might include pens, toothbrushes, toys, pillows, and cell phones.

**Weighted objects:** If your child has difficulty with his balance or his proprioceptive system, you can use a weighted object to help him. A weighted vest, back pack, fanny pack, or blanket can help your child feel more grounded and less concerned about his sense of movement. Deep pressure will help him calm down.

**Oral motor activities:** If your child has issues related to his mouth and to touch, blowing bubbles, eating crunchy foods, biting on a washcloth, and blowing a cotton ball across the table with a straw can help him satisfy his need for oral stimulation and movement.

# What Can I Do to Make Sure That My Child Does Not Go into Sensory Overload?

One of the most important things you can do is to make sure that the light throughout your home is not too bright. Fluorescent lights can be especially distracting. Look for ways you can use indirect lighting (lamps, for example), or at the very least, non-fluorescent overhead lights.

Make sure that the noise level in your home is not so loud that your child is unable to function. Watch for signs that your child is overwhelmed by the noise at home (he begins to look around the room nervously, begins fidgeting, or covers his ears with his hands). Provide a quiet place for him to get away from the noise.

When noise is unavoidable, it is very important that you prepare your child. For example, before you turn on the vacuum cleaner give your child a pair of headphones to wear.

**Avoid Sensory Overload**

- Use indirect lighting or non-fluorescent overhead lighting.
- Control the noise level.
- Use textures that are calming.
- Use mild, natural scents.

Consider the texture of the materials in your child's environment, and include items with textures that you know he might enjoy. If you know that your child likes soft textures, provide a soft surface for him to play on, such as a mat or craft foam. Using something as simple as a foam hair curler as a pencil grip can make all the difference in whether your child learns to write or avoids it. Your child may be able to sit and play a game if he sits on a beanbag chair or balances himself on a large therapy ball.

Be aware of the smells in your home. To you, the sweet smell of a rose-scented air freshener might be pleasing. However, it could interfere with your child's ability to function and, in extreme cases, could lead to an unwanted outburst. If you use scents, use natural ones, and then only after you have determined that your child can tolerate them. For example, try peppermint, lavender, or vanilla, instead of sweet and flowery scents.

---

The following pages outline a few ideas and strategies to help you address your child's sensory integration issues. These strategies are:

- Weighted Vest
- Snuggle Blanket
- Make a Fidgety-Widgety Toy
- Cocoon
- Stand-Up Pushups!

## Weighted Vest

The weight from the vest will help your child feel more comfortable, and, as a result, he will be able to focus more attentively on what he is doing.

### Materials

Smock with pockets, large shirt with pockets and the sleeves cut off, or child's vest; cloth for additional pockets; small cloth bags; salt, sand, or uncooked rice; needle and thread; Velcro (the kind that is sewed in place)

### What to Do

1. Use a smock with pockets or a large shirt with the sleeves cut off. A vest with pockets will also work.
2. Add two more pockets to the back of the shirt or smock. Place the back pockets in approximately the same place on the vest, shirt, or smock where the front pockets are located. The result is a vest with four pockets, two in the front and two in the back.
3. Make the weights by filling small cloth bags with salt, sand, or rice. Sew the bags shut. Each bag should weigh no more than four ounces. Place weights in vest pockets and Velcro the pockets shut.

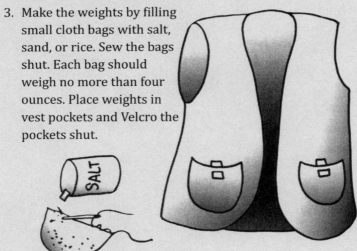

## Snuggle Blanket

Let your child use this snuggle blanket to wrap herself in as a way for her to calm down when things are overwhelming for her.

### Materials

3–4 yards of stretchy Lycra or spandex material (swimsuit material), needle and thread (or portable sewing machine)

### What to Do

1. Purchase three to four yards of Lycra or Spandex material.
2. Select a color and pattern that you know the child will enjoy.
3. Sew a small $^{1}/_{2}$"–1" hem around the material to keep it from fraying.
4. Keep the blanket in a location that is convenient for your child. She can retrieve the blanket and wrap up in it for comfort whenever she feels overwhelmed.

### Helpful Hint

■ Lycra or Spandex works best; however, you might experiment with other fabric.

## Make a Fidgety-Widgety Toy

Learning to control her behavior is a very important step in your child's social and emotional development. Use this strategy when you want to help your child learn to calm down.

### Materials
Deflated helium-type balloon; plastic sack; filler, such as flour or sand; soft cloth or material; tape

### What to Do
1. A fidgety-widgety is simply a toy that your child squeezes when she wants to remain calm.
2. To make it, fill a deflated helium-quality balloon or a sturdy, resealable plastic bag with flour or sand. Tie the end of the balloon or seal the plastic bag. If using a plastic bag, place it inside another plastic bag for added safety. Cover the balloon or bag with soft cloth and seal the end.
3. Introduce the toy to your child and demonstrate how to squeeze it. Encourage her to squeeze it, too.
4. Place the toy where your child can reach it when she needs it.
5. When the fidgety-widgety begins to wear out, it can be replaced easily.

### Helpful Hints
- Experiment with various textures, colors, and sizes.
- Make the toy small enough that your child can hold it in her hand.
- The fidgety-widgety is not designed to be a chew toy and should only be used in the presence of an adult.

STRATEGY

## Cocoon

If your child does not like to be touched, he may be comfortable with the deep pressure of this cocoon that may help him relax.

### Materials

Foam-type mat, lightweight sleeping bag, or rubber gym mat; a large, sturdy beach ball or therapy ball

### What to Do

1. Play a game with your child. Using deep, even pressure, press the ball up and down his body. Say something like, "We're pretending you are a caterpillar. We need to get you ready for your cocoon."
2. Say to your child, "Tell me when you want me to stop." Pause and see if he responds.
3. Next say, "Are you ready to get in your cocoon?" Gently, but firmly, roll your child up in the mat or sleeping bag. This is best accomplished by putting one hand on his shoulder and the other hand on his hip or leg. Never cover his head.
4. Rock your child back and forth a few times.
5. When your child is ready for you to stop, say, "Now we are going to pretend you are a butterfly."
6. Gently, unroll your child by grasping the edge of the mat. If possible, encourage him to unroll himself while you hold firmly to the mat.

### Helpful Hints

- This activity can be a fun and relaxing way to help your child cope with sensory overload.
- If your child does not want his whole body in the cocoon, try just his torso, hands, or feet.
- Safety is always the most important consideration. Never cover your child's head when rolling him up in the mat, and always remember that this activity requires adult supervision.

## Stand-Up Pushups!

This strategy is a way for your child to calm herself before she goes into sensory overload.

**Materials**
None

**What to Do**
1. Select a large, solid structure in the room or outside. A wall or a permanent structure works best.
2. Walk up to the wall and say, "I'm going to do some stand-up pushups."
3. Place your hands against the wall and count to 10.
4. Use varying amounts of pressure and smile at your child while you push against the wall.
5. Invite your child to join you in a stand-up pushup.

**Helpful Hints**
■ Remember, this activity requires adult supervision.
■ Encourage your child to try this with other parts of her body as well, such as her hips, back, or using her feet while lying down.

## For More Information

Arnwine, B. 2006. *Starting sensory integration therapy: Fun activities that won't destroy your home or classroom.* Arlington, TX: Future Horizons

Beil, L. & Peske, N. 2005. *Raising a sensory smart child: The definitive handbook for helping your child with sensory integration issues.* New York: Penquin

Isbell, C. & Isbell, R. 2008. *Sensory integration: A guide for preschool teachers.* Beltsville, MD: Gryphon House.

Kranowitz, C.S. 2003. *The out-of-sync child has fun: Safe activities for home and school—sensory-motor, appropriate, fun, and easy.* New York: The Berkley Publishing Group.

Williamson, G.G. & Anzalone, M.E. 2001. *Sensory integration and self-regulation in infants and toddlers: Helping very young children interact with their environment.* Washington DC: Zero to Three.

# Key Terms

**Hypersensitive:** Overly sensitive to sensory stimulation.

**Hyposensitive:** Under-sensitive to sensory stimulation.

**Proprioceptive sense:** The sense that receives information from joints, muscles, and ligaments, providing information about where parts of the body are and what they are doing.

**Sensory Integration Dysfunction (SI Dysfunction):** A condition resulting from an insufficient process in the brain, whereby your child is unable to analyze and respond appropriately to the information received from the senses.

**Vestibular sense:** The sense that provides information through the inner ear about balance, movement (inner ear), and gravity.

# Chapter 5

# Helping Your Child Learn to Be Independent

*Some parents get excited over the first step or the first word;
for us it was the first time Kristen sat at the table
without a tantrum.*
—Rita and Chuck, the parents of Kristen

## What Are Life Skills?

Life skills, also known as self-help skills, everyday skills, independent-living skills, and functional skills, are the skills that your child will use throughout his life. They are skills that will help him become more independent, including going to the bathroom, feeding himself, dressing himself, brushing his teeth, taking a bath, and learning to recognize common things around him such as restrooms, exits, and stop signs. As your child gets older, these skills might include learning to access community resources, such as the bank, post office, and grocery store.

# Why Are Life Skills Important?

Predictability and routines are very important to children with autism, and the more they are able to take care of their own personal needs, the more predictable their daily life will be. Additionally, learning to take care of basic needs such as going to the bathroom, washing, and dressing will help your child socially. Other children are more likely to want to interact and play with a child with good personal hygiene. Most importantly, life skills help your child's self-esteem, by giving him a sense of accomplishment and the confidence that comes from doing it "all by himself."

# How Do I Help My Child Learn to Do Everyday Tasks (Life Skills)?

Work with your child's teacher and school to determine which life skills your child should learn first. When helping your child learn any skill, it is important that you and your child's teacher use the same methods and practice the same skill in exactly the same way. Using the same words, phrases, and picture cues reinforces the new skill, making it easier to learn.

It is important that your child learn and practice life skills in the context of daily routines and in the environment in which that skill would likely happen. For example, you would not want your child to learn to brush his teeth by practicing with an imaginary toothbrush. Instead, you would take him to the natural environment, in this case the bathroom, where brushing his teeth would normally happen. Remember that children with autism are very literal, and practicing a skill in a time or place in which that skill would not normally occur is confusing and slows down his progress in developing that skill. Because your child is so busy trying to figure out why something is being practiced in a simulated or pretend way, he often fails to concentrate on what you are asking him to do. This chapter focuses on just those skills that will help your child in his day-to-day routines.

Life skills fall into these categories:
- **Feeding**
—Using utensils to eat
—Using simple table rules
—Knowing the social context of mealtime
- **Toileting**
—Asking to go to the toilet
—Taking care of his own toilet needs
—Washing her hands after toileting
- **Handling Unplanned Situations**
- **Self-Care**
—Brushing his teeth
—Washing and drying her face
—Tolerating a bath
- **Dressing**
—Getting dressed for school
—Getting dressed to go outside
—Taking off and putting on clothes
—Learning to select clothes appropriate for the weather
- **Simple Routines**
—Getting up in the morning
—Arriving at school
—Learning the daily routine
—Getting ready to go to lunch
—Getting ready to go home

- Adjusting to school after a period of being out of school (after vacation, illness, and so on)

# What Do I Do First?

Deciding which skill to work on first with your child depends on information from a variety of sources and on the developmental level of your child. Begin by looking at some general guidelines to use when planning to work on developing any new skill.

- **Start by deciding which skill is the most appropriate for your child at this stage of development.** This decision should be based on the developmental level of your child and on your careful observation of your child. Trying to help your child develop a life skill before he is ready can be confusing, frustrating, and frightening for the child, and may make it difficult for her to learn the skill.

- **Identify the challenges your child may have with learning the skill you have selected**, such as if your child is hyper-sensitive to touch, has a short attention span, or is unwilling to tolerate certain elements in the environment, such as water.

> Trying to help your child learn a life skill before she is ready can be confusing, frustrating, and frightening for her.

- **Tell everyone who interacts with your child** so they are aware that he is learning something new. Don't forget to include your child's teacher, after-school caregiver, and other people with whom your child spends a significant amount of time.

- **Gather all the materials** your child will need to learn the new skill.

- **Make a list of the words you are using to help your child learn the new skill**. Be sure to check with your child's teacher so that you are both using the same words and the same procedure for practicing the new skill. Children with autism do best with concrete terms; make sure you are using terms that are not confusing.

- **Make a step-by-step guide for completing the skill**. Write down each step and then go over the list to see if you have left off anything important. On your list, be very detailed and describe for yourself what you want your child to do.

- **Make another step-by-step guide that you will use with the child.** This list is much less detailed and simpler than the list you made for yourself. Be very specific, concise, and clear about what your child is to do.

- **Practice the skill several times yourself**, using the list you have made for your child. Watch yourself as you model each step. Remember, things that seem natural to you, such as hanging up a towel after you use it or flushing a toilet, may not be natural for your child.

- **Figure out the best time for your child to begin to start learning the new skill**. Even if your child is not ready to do the complete task alone, she still may be ready to start learning some of the basic steps.

- **Make sequence cards for each step** and use simple pictures that clearly demonstrate what you are doing.

Make a second set of cards to send with her to school. It is always good to make a third set of cards as a back-up, in case something happens to the sequence cards.

- **Practice any new skill in the environment in which it would occur**. For example, the child should practice tooth brushing at a real sink in the bathroom—not at a pretend sink. Your child should learn feeding skills when she is eating, and so on. Place the sequence cards in front of your child and talk about each one. Remember to use clear, concrete language.

- **Model each step for the child** before asking her to start the task.

- **Don't forget the home-school connection.** Keep your child's school involved so that her teacher can reinforce at school what she is learning at home. It may be difficult for your child to apply what she learned at home to a similar situation at school without help from her teacher.

- **Give your child time to practice one step of a skill** before going on to the next. Expecting too much too soon can be overwhelming for both you and your child.

**How to Help Your Child Learn a New Skill**

- Start by deciding which skill is the most important to your child and your family.
- Identify the challenges to teaching the skill you have selected.
- Inform everyone who will be working with your child that you plan to help your child learn something new.
- Gather all the materials your child will need to learn the new skill.
- Make a list of the words you will use to help your child learn the new skill.
- Make a step-by-step guide for completing the skill. Write down each step and then go over the list to see if you forgot anything important.
- Make another step-by-step guide for your child that is much less detailed than the list you made for yourself.
- Practice the skill several times by yourself using the list you have made for your child.
- Figure out the best time to begin implementing the new skill.
- Make sequence cards for each step and use simple pictures that clearly demonstrate what you are doing. Make a second set of cards to send to your child's school.
- Practice any new skill in the environment in which it would occur.
- Keep your child's school involved.
- Don't be discouraged if your child is unable to transfer a new skill from one environment to another (from home to school).
- Give your child time to practice one step of a skill before going on to a new skill.

# How Does This All Fit Together?

How can you apply this information to a specific skill, such as brushing teeth? Let's look at Terrance, a four-year-old with autism, who is not upset by water; in fact, his mother has noticed that he enjoys watching water as it comes out of the faucet. His mother talks to his teacher and his grandmother, who takes care of him after school. Together, they determine that brushing his teeth independently is an important skill for Terrance to learn. His mother is concerned because Terrance's other brothers and sisters have had dental problems in the past, and she wants him to have healthy teeth. Terrance's mother does the following: She gathers the materials Terrance will need to begin learning this new skill: a toothbrush, toothpaste, and a plastic cup. Terrance's mother talks with his teacher and grandmother and they decide they will start helping Terrance learn to brush his teeth the following day. They make a list of the vocabulary words they will use while Terrance learns this skill.

Vocabulary Words to Use When Terrance Learns to Brush His Teeth:

| | |
|---|---|
| toothbrush | rinse |
| toothpaste | teeth |
| lid (top for toothpaste) | mouth |
| inside | top |
| outside | bottom |

**Note:** Terrance's mother decides not to use the word cap for the top of the toothpaste, because she knows that Terrance is very literal and may be confused because he uses the word cap for the hat he wears on his head.

After reviewing the word list, Terrance's mother decides that Terrance will need to review the concepts of *inside*, *outside*, *top*, and *bottom*, before he learns the steps to brushing his teeth independently. Next, she writes down all the steps Terrance will need to learn to do the task successfully.

The step-by-step guide for tooth brushing:
1. Tell Terrance it is time to brush his teeth.
2. Walk into the bathroom with Terrance.
3. Turn on the faucet.
4. Run water over the toothbrush.
5. Pick up the toothpaste and open the lid.
6. Put a small amount of toothpaste on the toothbrush.
7. Set the toothbrush down, being careful not to let the toothpaste touch any unclean surfaces.
8. Put the lid on the toothpaste.
9. Pick up the toothbrush and lift it to his mouth.
10. Brush his front teeth.
11. Brush his back teeth.
12. Brush the teeth on top of his mouth.
13. Brush the teeth at the bottom of his mouth.
14. Spit out the toothpaste and turn on water to rinse it down the drain.
15. Put the toothbrush down.
16. Pick up the glass of water.
17. Rinse the inside of his mouth and spit out the water.
18. Clean the toothbrush and put it in a sanitary container.
19. Wipe his mouth with a clean cloth or paper towel.

Terrance's mother walks through each step several times and practices modeling each for him. She simplifies the list by making a picture schedule. The following day, she shows the picture schedule to Terrance and they practice each step together.

The hardest part for Terrance is learning to turn off the water after he has rinsed the sink. However, with practice, he learns to stop watching the water go down the drain and return his attention to finishing the sequence. After two months, Terrance can brush his teeth with only minimal assistance from an adult.

Terrance became so familiar with the process of brushing his teeth that he learned to complete each step with only minimal assistance. To help him remember the parts that were most difficult, his mother held up a picture from his picture schedule to remind him.

The following pages outline a few ideas and strategies to help you child learn self-help skills. These strategies are:
- Communicating a Need to Go to the Bathroom
- Making Toileting Work
- Bathroom Detective: When Your Child Gets Upset in the Bathroom
- Mealtime Fun!
- Learning to Put on Socks and Shoes
- Personal Information
- Hand Washing
- Crossing the Street

## Communicating a Need to Go to the Bathroom

Use this strategy to help your child with toilet training. This strategy is not effective after your child has already had an accident.

**Materials**
None

**What to Do**

1. Begin by learning the American Sign Language sign for *bathroom*. This is a very simple sign to learn. Make a fist and insert the thumb between the second and third finger. Move the hand up and down. This sign is very effective, quickly learned, and alleviates the need for your child to ask aloud to go to the bathroom.

2. Once you have learned the sign, begin to use it every time your child goes to the bathroom. Make the sign and say, "_____(Your child's name), you need to go to the bathroom."

3. Remember that when your child is first learning a new sign, his attempt to make the sign may be similar but not exactly like the one you want him to use. This is called *approximation*. It is okay for your child to approximate a sign. However, continue to model for him how to make it correctly.

4. Meet with your child's teacher and encourage him or her to use the sign with your child as well, even if your child is verbal or uses pictures to communicate. Using this sign can be very effective in his overall toilet-training routine.

## Making Toileting Work

Use this strategy to teach your child toileting skills, not when she has already had an accident or if she consistently refuses to use the bathroom.

### Materials

Picture schedule for going to the bathroom

### What to Do

1. Make a list of words that you will use: *potty, bathroom, pee-pee, poo-poo, paper, flush*, and so on. Make sure the words you use are the same words that your child uses at school. For example, if you say, "Do you need to go the *bathroom*?" and at school the teacher says, "Do you need to go to the *restroom*?" then your child will likely become confused. Talk with your child's teacher and decide what words will be used for urinate and defecate. It is not a good idea to use the terms "number 1" and "number 2," as these are too abstract.

2. Brainstorm ideas and gather materials that will help your child be successful. For example, a child with tactile sensitivity will need to use very soft toilet paper. Keep in mind that once your child learns the routine, she will need practice going to the bathroom in both familiar and unfamiliar settings.

3. Make going to the bathroom a part of the everyday routine. Include a picture on your child's daily picture schedule. Later, after your child learns to associate the picture with going to the bathroom, she can walk to the picture and point when she needs to go.

4. Write out each step of the process for yourself. These notes are for you, so be specific and detailed. Make a list of what will happen first, second, and so on.

5. Make a picture schedule for going to the bathroom. Use pictures that are very specific and easily understood. Line drawings often work better than detailed color pictures.

6. Go over the picture schedule with your child before going to the bathroom. Make a game out of the activity. Talk about what happens first, what happens second, and so on.

7. Take your child to the bathroom and go through each step with her. It may be necessary for you to model for her what to do, such as pulling up her pants after she finishes or drying her hands after she washes them.

8. Encourage your child to be as independent as possible; remember that success requires consistency, patience, and practice.

9. Be sure to praise your child for any successful attempt. Remember, the goal is for the child to learn to use the toilet independently. Communicating that she needs to go is a separate goal.

**Helpful Hints**

■ Encouraging the child to drink water or other liquid prior to practicing this routine is often helpful.

■ Children with autism may have additional issues with the bathroom, such as fear of sitting on the toilet, avoidance of touching toilet paper or of wiping themselves, a need to flush over and over, and a resistance to change, which may include a resistance to giving up wearing a diaper.

■ Because children with autism don't always adapt well to new settings, anticipate that though your child may be perfectly trained to use the toilet at home, she may hesitate to use unfamiliar bathrooms.

## Bathroom Detective: When Your Child Gets Upset in the Bathroom

Use this strategy after you have had some success with toilet training. It may help you figure out why your child resists going to the bathroom or why he gets upset when going to the bathroom.

**Materials**
Bathroom Checklist (see the following page)

**What to do**
1. Try to determine the root cause of the bathroom problem. Start by looking for the obvious. Knowing that children with autism require very set routines, ask yourself the following question: What was different today? Perhaps a different family member took your child to the bathroom.
2. Look at other factors as well. Did you insist that your child go when he was involved in a favorite activity? Did you make him go at a time that was different than when you asked him to go yesterday?
3. Immediately following the incident, take a trip to the bathroom yourself. Use the Bathroom Checklist to help you.
4. If you did not take your child to the bathroom, interview the person who did. Explain to this person that you just need information to help you determine what went wrong.
5. Accept the fact that you may never really know what went wrong, and try again later.

## Bathroom Checklist

| Questions | Comments |
|---|---|
| Look around the bathroom. Does it look physically the same as it did the day before? Even a small change such as a new tissues or towels can be distracting. | |
| Is the temperature or lighting in the bathroom different? | |
| Is the toilet paper the same as yesterday? If not, what is different about it? | |
| Is there an unfamiliar or new odor in the bathroom? Even the addition of a new air freshener can be upsetting for a child with autism. | |
| Can you see anything else that may be different from the last time your child used the restroom? | |

### Helpful Hints

- If your child continues to be resistant, check with his teachers to see if he is having a problem at school as well.
- The problem may be unrelated to the bathroom itself; your child may not feel well or may be constipated.

## Mealtime Fun!

Use this strategy to make mealtime an enjoyable experience for your child and your family. It is effective when you have had time to discuss your child's food issues, mealtime preferences, and other meal-related issues with other family members.

### Materials

Poster board or construction paper in the child's favorite color, laminating materials or clear contact paper, markers for drawing on the mat

### What to Do

1. Observe your child during a meal, using the Mealtime/Snack Observation Checklist on page 110. Pay close attention to other factors, such as whether he prefers to sit in the same seat each day, whether he eats more consistently when food is presented on a plate with divided compartments, and whether he asks for more if he wants more to eat.

2. Using the checklist as a guide, look at your child's preferences when planning the mealtime routine.

3. Be sure to tell your child a few minutes before it is time to eat. This will allow him to get ready for meals. Consider showing your child a picture that depicts eating.

4. Model for your child how to ask for more. If he is nonverbal, teach him the sign for *more*.

more

5. Make a placemat using the child's favorite color. The mat can be made of poster board or construction paper and laminated. On the placemat, draw the outline of each

utensil in the proper place—draw a large circle for your child's plate and a smaller one for his cup.

6. Encourage your child to be as independent as possible at mealtime, but recognize that he may experience distress about eating and may refuse to eat or to try new foods.

**Helpful Hints**

- Don't force your child to try to new foods.
- If possible, reduce the light level and use indirect lighting during mealtime.
- Spills are a natural part of eating. If your child spills something and gets upset, talk quietly and assure him that everything is just fine.
- Sometimes, children with autism get so upset that they throw food or plates on the floor. When this happens, ask your child if he is finished eating and redirect him while you clean up the spill.
- Make mealtime as relaxing as possible. Play soft music or talk quietly with your child while you eat.

**Mealtime/Snack Observation Checklist**

Observe your child periodically. Use the Mealtime/Snack Observation Checklist on the following page to help monitor your child's progress. If your child is inconsistent in a specific area, check the box that says *sometimes*. Write any comments that are helpful in the box beside each question.

## Mealtime/Snack Observation Checklist

| Ask Yourself | Yes | No | Sometimes | Comments |
|---|---|---|---|---|
| Does your child sit in the same chair during meals? | | | | |
| Does your child sit by the same person each time he eats? | | | | |
| Does your child use utensils when she eats? | | | | |
| Will your child let one food touch another? | | | | |
| Does your child eat a variety of foods? | | | | |
| Will your child try new foods? | | | | |
| Does your child seem to have a mealtime ritual (folding napkin a certain way, arranging his plate a certain way, and so on)? | | | | |
| Does your child let you know if she wants more? | | | | |
| Does your child let you know if he is finished? | | | | |

## Learning to Put on Socks and Shoes

Use this strategy to help your child learn how to put on her socks and shoes independently with minimal assistance or prompting. It is not effective when your child is agitated, anxious, or upset.

### Materials

Picture cards (3 or 4) depicting the steps to putting on socks and shoes

### What to Do

1. Make a list of the steps that your child needs to follow to put on her socks and shoes. Decide if you are going to teach her to put on both socks, then both shoes, or if you are going to complete putting the sock and shoe on one foot before going to the other one.
2. Make a step-by-step guide for your child to follow.
3. See if your child will let you model each step for her, using your own socks and shoes. Ask her to watch you. Then, she should try it herself.
4. Praise your child for attempting to put on her own socks and shoes.
5. Make a series of three or four picture cards to help remind your child of the correct sequence in the activity. Most children have shoes that are attached with Velcro, so tying shoes is not an issue.
6. If your child appears to be sensitive about the socks or gets anxious, make sure they are on her foot properly. Children with autism often tend to be very sensitive when material is scratchy or does not fit properly.

## Personal Information

Use this strategy to teach your child to say or show personal information when asked. This is a critical survival strategy, and it is never too soon to plan for an emergency.

### Materials

Pictures of community helpers who may assist during an emergency, such as police officers, firefighters, nurses, doctors, and others

### What to Do

1. Begin by explaining to your child that you are going to teach him a song. Tell him that if he is ever lost or has an emergency he can sing this song.
2. Explain that an emergency is a situation where he can't find you or his teachers, or when he is lost.
3. Show your child pictures of firefighters, police officers, and other emergency workers (be sure to include nurses and doctors). Tell your child that if he ever needs help, he should look for someone in a uniform.
4. Teach the child the following song, sung to the tune of "The Farmer in the Dell:"

   **My Name**
   *My name is ____* (insert child's first name),
   *My name is ____* (insert child's first name),
   *My name is ____* (insert child's first name)
   *And I live on ____* (insert name of the child's street).

5. Practice the song often and begin each time by saying, "We are going to sing this song. If you ever have an emergency and need help, you can sing this song."
6. Review the list of helpers and show the pictures again, before singing the song.

7. After your child learns the first verse, teach him the next verse:

*My ____ 's* (insert name of a person living with you, such as mom, dad, or other adult) *name is ____.*
*My ____ 's* (insert name of a person living with you, such as mom, dad, or other adult) *name is ____.*
*My ____ 's* (insert name of a person living with you, such as mom, dad, or other adult) *name is ____.*
*We live at ____* (complete address).

For example:
*My mom's name is Sheila McDonald.*
*My mom's name is Sheila McDonald.*
*My mom's name is Sheila McDonald.*
*We live at 1400 West 34th Street.*

Or, teach him the following variation:

*I live with my grandmother.*
*I live with my grandmother.*
*I live with my grandmother.*
*Her name is Clara Brownlow.*

**Helpful Hints**
- Be sure to send a copy of the song to school and encourage your child's teacher to talk about and practice the song with your child.
- Remember that it is most likely your child will have an emergency when he is away from home, so make sure all the people who know and work with your child use the song often.
- Review both the song and the community helpers who can come to your child's aid if there is an emergency.

## Hand Washing

Use this strategy to teach your child a routine to wash her hands independently. It is not effective if your child is resistant to water and throws a tantrum when asked to place her hands under water.

**Materials**
None

**What to Do**
Picture sequence cards are always helpful, but this strategy depends on modeling what you want your child to do.

1. Walk with your child to the sink.
2. Tell her that you are going to play a game where you do something and then she does the same thing.
3. Say, "First, we turn on the water." Turn on the water. (Wait to see if your child turns on the faucet, too.)
4. Say, "Now, we get some soap." Put some soap on your hands. (Wait to see if your child puts soap on her hands.)
5. Say, "Next, we put our hands under the water." Put your hands under the water, and wait to see if your child does the same thing.
6. Say, "Now, we rub our hands together and count to 10." Rub soap on your hands and count to 10.
7. Say, "Next, we rinse the soap off our hands." (Wait to see if your child rinses her hands. If she does not, repeat the instructions.)
8. Say, "Now, we dry our hands." Reach for a towel and dry your hands.
9. Say, "Finally, we put the towel back where we found it."

## Crossing the Street

Use this strategy to teach your child how to cross a street independently. It is not effective when your child is absorbed in a favorite activity.

**Materials**
None

**What to Do**
1. Even though an adult will probably be present when your child crosses the street, it is still important that he learn what to do.
2. Use this strategy when you are crossing a real street; even the bus lane at your child's school is a street. Practice outside, so that your child learns to associate this strategy with crossing the street.
3. Teach your child the following song, sung to the tune of "Three Blind Mice."

*Stop, listen, look,*
*Stop, listen, look,*
*When you cross the street,*
*When you cross the street.*
*Look to the left and then to the right.*
*Look to the left and then to the right.*
*Remember, every time you cross the street to*
*Stop, listen, look.*
*Stop, listen, look.*

4. Practice the song several times, crossing the street as you sing.

## For More Information

Abrams, P. & L. Henriques. 2004. *The autistic spectrum: Parent's daily helper*. Berkeley, CA: Ulysses Press.

Baker, B. L., & A. J. Brightman. 2003. *Steps to independence: Teaching everyday skills to children with special needs*. Baltimore, MD: Paul H. Brookes.

Coucouvanis, J. 2008. *The potty journey: Guide to toilet training children with special needs including autism and related disorders*. Shawnee Mission, KS: Autism Asperger Publishing Company.

Small, M. & L. Kontente. 2003. *Everyday solutions: A practical guide for families of children with autism spectrum disorders*. Shawnee Mission, KS: Autism Asperger Publishing Company.

Wheeler, M. 2007. *Toilet training for individuals with autism or other developmental issues (second edition)*. Arlington, TX: Future Horizons.

## Key Terms

**Approximation**: An inexact representation of a skill or a word that is still close enough to be useful.

**Functional skills:** Everyday skills that your child will use to be more independent, also called self-help skills, life skills, or independent-living skills. Functional skills are the skills your child will use throughout his life, such as brushing his teeth, going to the bathroom, and taking a bath.

**Hyper-sensitivity:** Overly sensitive to something, the state of being overly stimulated by the environment.

**Reverse chaining:** When your child starts at the end of an activity and does the process in reverse. For example, when your child is learning to put on his coat, in reverse chaining you would start with taking off the coat.

**Task analysis:** The breaking down of a skill into steps; a step-by-step guide.

# Chapter 6

# Your Child in Your Community

*Our main goal for Christopher is that he be given the same opportunities to learn as other children.*
*—Paul, the father of Christopher*

## How Do I Prepare My Child for School?

The best way to prepare your child for school is to get to know as much as possible about your child's school and his new teacher before he begins school. Take your child to visit his new classroom before the first day of school. This initial visit will give you time to get to know the teacher and give your child time to become familiar with his classroom. This visit should happen when other children are not present.

To help your child get ready for his new classroom, additional visits may be necessary. Although most preschools already have a parent information form, you will need to provide much more information for his teacher than is usually included on a simple form.

Most children will go to a preschool setting with an Individual Education Plan (IEP) or an Individual Family Service Plan

(IFSP) already in place. However, those plans are designed to look at broad educational objectives and goals for your child and may have been written long before he arrives at school. The IEP or the IFSP is a good tool to help your child's school plan the curriculum for him. However, the school will also need to know as much as possible about your child and his preferences and experiences with others so that when he arrives they are prepared. If he was previously in a preschool or child care facility, schedule a visit with his teacher. Ideally, she would come with him when he visits a new class for the first time. Your goal as the parent is to make his transition from the previous setting to a new classroom as stress-free as possible for both you and your child.

## What Should I Look for When Selecting a School for My Child?

The environment should be as well-defined as possible. Each center or learning area should be clearly marked with a picture. It is also very important that the teacher be willing to include a picture schedule in each area so your child can look at the schedule and begin to learn what is supposed to occur within that area. This will reduce anxiety. Remember, your child may like to know what he is supposed to do, so a picture schedule is reassuring and will help him adjust to his new classroom.

Your child also needs a special place that is located in the quietest part of the room, without distractions, where he can get away from the noise and activity in the classroom. This quiet place should have indirect soft lighting, a chair or cushion that is comfortable for your child, and a few activities that your child likes. It is also a place where your child can go to complete activities that are especially stressful for him.

Keep in mind when selecting a new school or a specific classroom for your child that children with autism function best when they have:

- Structure,
- A predictable routine,
- Environments that are not distracting,
- Verbal reminders of what will happen next, and
- Picture schedules of the day's activities.

# Your Child in the Community

Your child may find that visiting a new place, meeting new people, or being asked to participate in a new activity is overwhelming. To help your child manage these situations keep in mind the following:

1. The key to success is preparing your child by helping him know what to expect in the new environment.
2. Use pictures to reinforce where you are going and what might happen when you arrive.
3. Remember that children with autism function better when they are rested and when sensory stimulation is kept at a minimum.
4. Start gradually by spending a few minutes in the new environment, and then build up to a longer interval.
5. Prepare for the unexpected. No matter how well you plan, unexpected events will occur.
6. Even if the initial trip to a place in your community was unsuccessful, don't give up. Just because your child had difficulty once does not mean he will always have difficulty.

Children with autism need concrete information about what is expected in a given environment. Don't assume your child knows what to do in a fast-food restaurant, the library, or the grocery store.

---

The following pages outline a few ideas and strategies to help your child learn to adjust to preschool. These strategies are:

- Before School Starts: A Strategy to Help Your Child's Teacher
- Good Morning! Good Morning!: A Strategy to Start the Day
- Eating Out
- Going to the Store

## Before School Starts: A Strategy to Help Your Child's Teacher

Use this strategy to help your child feel comfortable and confident in school. This strategy works best if you can use it the first day your child is in school.

**Materials**
Notebook or folder for taking notes during the meeting

**What to Do**
1. Provide your child's teacher with a copy of your child's most recent medical evaluation.
2. Contact the school to arrange a meeting with your child's teacher. When you meet your child's teacher, be positive and tell her you are excited about having your child (use his name) in that teacher's class. Assure the teacher that you want to meet to plan for his success in preschool together, and that you are looking forward to being a team member with them.
3. When meeting with your child's teacher, invite grandparents, babysitters, or extended family members to go along with you.
4. Remember to take notes throughout the meeting. Jot down any questions you might want to ask before the meeting ends.

**Helpful Hint**
■ Focus on your child's abilities, rather than his disabilities.

## Good Morning! Good Morning! A Strategy to Start the Day

This strategy is a gentle way to wake up and to start getting dressed.

### Materials

Picture schedule of morning wakeup routine, which may include getting up, going to the bathroom, brushing teeth, or getting dressed

### What to Do

1. It is important to start each day with the same routine. Use the same words and phrases each day, such as, "Good morning, (your child's name)," and then wait to see if your child responds. "Let's see what we will do first."
2. You should either kneel down at your child's eye level and show her a picture schedule of what you want her to do or point out to your child what happens first.
3. If your child does not respond to a spoken good morning, she may respond to a song such as the following, sung to the tune of "Three Blind Mice" (first verse).

*Good morning, (your child's name),*
*Good morning, (your child's name),*
*Time to wake up. Time to wake up.*
*First you're going to _____ (get out of bed, brush your teeth)*
*And next you're going to _____*
*Good morning, (your child's name),*
*Good morning, (your child's name),*

4. Next, direct your child to the first thing on the picture schedule. If she hesitates, walk with her, show her what to do, and then say or sign, "Thank you."

## Eating Out

This strategy helps you prepare your child to eat in a restaurant with your family.

### Materials

Pictures of the types of food served in the restaurant where you will be eating (many fast-food restaurants have children's menus with pictures of the food choices available for children)

1. Select a restaurant and visit it before going with your child. If your child has sensory integration issues, remember to check the lighting and noise level. For the first visit, choose a time when the restaurant is less crowded so the wait time for food is minimized.
2. Talk to your child before you leave so he knows where you are going and what to expect when you arrive. Use the menu from the restaurant to help your child select what he might order. If your child is non-verbal, make a picture list of what he wants to order so he can present it at the restaurant.
3. Drive by the restaurant ahead of time and begin to talk to your child about going there to eat.
4. The unexpected often happens, so be prepared. If your first trip is unsuccessful, try to determine what factors you could change to make subsequent trips more enjoyable for you and your child. (For example, is there a better time of day to go, is there a better place to sit in the restaurant, or can you make your child feel more comfortable by bringing his favorite plate from home to eat on.)
5. Have a contingency plan, such as taking another adult with you, should your child become upset and need to go outside for a few minutes. One adult can go outside with your child while the other stays inside. If it is necessary to leave the restaurant with your child, return as soon as possible.

## Going to the Grocery Store

Going to the store can be overwhelming. The sights, smells, light, and noise can lead to sensory overload. Minimize the impact by keeping shopping trips short and by involving your child in the process of selecting groceries.

### Materials

Plain index cards, glue, pictures of food

### What to Do

1. If possible, select a time when the store is less crowded. If your child has tactile issues and resists sitting on the cold, hard metal of the seat in a shopping cart, take a blanket or towel for her to sit on.
2. Tell your child where you are going to take her and describe what will happen when you get there.
3. If there is a particular treat she enjoys, mention that as well. For example, "Remember when we go by the bakery, they always give you a free cookie."
4. Involve your child is the shopping. If you are selecting a food such as ketchup or olives, hold up two jars and ask her which one she likes best. Thank her for helping.
5. Talk to your child while you shop. For example, mention her favorite cereal as you put it into the basket.
6. If your child grabs things and tries to put them into the basket, hold your hand up, palm out, and say, "Stop." Then take the item away and place it back on the shelf.
7. When you arrive at the checkout stand, invite your child to help you place items on the counter.

## For More Information

Cohen, J. 2006. *Guns a'blazing: How parents of children on the autism spectrum and schools can work together without a shot being fired.* Shawnee Mission, KS: Autism Asperger Publishing Company.

Janzen, J. E., & Therapy Skills Builders. 2000. *Autism: Facts and strategies for parents.* New York: Elsevier Science.

McClannahan, L. E., & P. J. Krantz. 1998. *Activity schedules for children with autism: Teaching independent behavior.* Bethesda, MD: Woodbine House.

Zysk, V. & Notbohm, E. 2004. *1001 great ideas for teaching and raising children on the autism spectrum disorders.* Arlington, TX: Bright Horizons.

## Key Terms

**Picture schedule:** A series of pictures showing what is supposed to occur within an area or time-frame.

**Transition:** Moving from one activity or time of day to another, or in a classroom moving from one part of the daily schedule to another.

# Chapter 7

# Helping Your Child Get Along with Others

*Social skills seemed so easy for my other children, but with Rachel she struggles with being around other children. She wants to play but she doesn't seem to know what to do or when to do it.*
*—Tamera, the mother of Rachel*

## Why Are Social Skills Important?

Social skills are essential life skills that include the ability to make friends, knowing how to treat other people and how to interact socially, and knowing how to collaborate with other children. Most children with autism have considerable difficulty behaving appropriately in social situations. In fact, one of the defining characteristics of autism is an inability to see situations from someone else's point of view.

Children with autism don't develop social skills in the same way as their peers. While typically developing children learn social skills through observation and experience, children with autism struggle with social cues and are frequently unable to establish lasting social relationships. To understand how to help your child learn social skills, it is important to know about the stages of social development.

# What Are the Stages of Social Development?

Social development depends on many factors. For example, how often your child plays with other children and whether there are other siblings in the family are contributing factors in your child's ability to interact socially. In general, social development happens with cognitive and emotional development. As your child matures, his social relationships will become more complex. The following chart summarizes the major characteristics in the social development of children between two and five years old.

**Major Characteristics of Social Development**

| Approximate Age of Child | Primary Social Characteristics |
| --- | --- |
| Two years old | <ul><li>Plays alone</li><li>Is egocentric and self-absorbed</li><li>Depends on adults for guidance</li><li>May socialize to get something, but has little understanding of the feelings and needs of others</li></ul> |
| Three years old | <ul><li>Begins to learn to take turns</li><li>Begins to know the difference between girls and boys</li><li>Enjoys simple group activities</li><li>Likes to help with small chores</li><li>Responds to adult approval or disapproval</li></ul> |

**Major Characteristics of Social Development** *(cont'd.)*

| Approximate Age of Child | Primary Social Characteristics |
|---|---|
| Three years old (continued) | ■ Has a rudimentary understanding of empathy and the point of view of others |
| Four years old | ■ Becomes very social and plays simple games with rules<br>■ Selects a peer and might even play exclusively with that peer<br>■ Understands more fully that others have feelings and needs<br>■ Responds when someone else is unhappy or sad |
| Five years old | ■ Enjoys and takes pride in accomplishments<br>■ Will play with friends and shows a distinct preference for specific friends<br>■ Understands the abstract nature of social interactions<br>■ Can usually tell the difference between a kidding remark and a remark that is serious<br>■ Laughs and shows emotional responses freely |

# How Do I Teach Social Skills to My Child?

Most children learn social skills through experience and observation. They watch how other children act and what other children do in social settings. Then, based on their observations, they imitate the behavior of others. For children with autism, it is not as easy as that. They often lack the ability to learn social skills through observation or to interpret social cues. While many children are likely to benefit from observing a social situation, your child usually needs more. He must learn techniques that will help him respond appropriately in social settings. One technique that helps children with autism learn social skills is the use of stories that are written for your child to help him remember what to do in a given situation. These stories are often referred to as social scripts.

# What Are Social Scripts?

Social scripts are based on the concept by Carol Gray in which children observe appropriate social behaviors in the context of a story. Each story includes answers to questions that your child needs to know in order to interact with others. In other words, a social story answers who, what, when, where, and why questions about social interaction. In some senses, a social story can teach your child to respond to others, even if he does not fully understand why he is doing so. By simply imitating in real-life what happened in the story, your child begins to experience some semblance of social interaction with a peer.

Stories about social skills will help your child learn to predict how others might act in a social situation by giving him a better understanding of the thoughts, feelings, and points of view of other children. Social stories also will help your child learn more about what might be expected of him in such a setting. However, before deciding how to use social stories, it is important to observe your child and decide which of the three types of social challenges applies to your child.

# What Are the Three Types of Social Challenges?

The first type of social challenge is a socially avoidant child, who may try to escape a social situation by having a tantrum, being aggressive toward others, or hiding in a closet. Some children are socially avoidant because the environment has become too much for them—the noise, smells, and lights are more than they can stand. The only way they know how to react is to escape the situation altogether.

The second type of social challenge includes children who are socially indifferent. Although they may not avoid socialization by withdrawing or getting upset, they do not actively attempt to interact with others. Children in this category are happier being alone and have considerable difficulty making and keeping friends. A socially indifferent child allows social interactions to go on around him while remaining passive and not attempting to join in the interaction.

**Three Types of Social Challenges**

1. Socially avoidant
2. Socially indifferent
3. Socially awkward

Social awkwardness is the defining characteristic of the final type of social challenge. These children tend to be higher-functioning. For example, many children with Asperger's Syndrome fit into this category. While they will interact socially, their conversations seem to be centered on subjects of interest to them. They may talk about something they like but fail to respond when another child wants to change the subject or offer a comment. Socially awkward children do not understand the rules of polite conversation and can't grasp the concept of small talk. The general rule for children in this category is, "If it is not about something that interests me, it is not worth talking about." Socially awkward children probably benefit the most from the use of social stories.

## How Do I Write a Social Story?

Once you determine which social challenge applies to your child, it is time to begin observing your child. General guidelines for observing your child include:

- Observing your child on multiple occasions and in a variety of settings,
- Making careful notes about his interests and preferences,
- Making a list of the children he plays with most often, and
- Determining if there are certain activities, toys, or people that upset him.

Before writing a social story, it is always a good idea to ask other people (teachers, therapists) who work with your child about what they have noticed about him in social situations. Compare their observations with yours. Next, decide on which social skill you want to work on first, keeping in mind that your child may have social difficulties because he cannot understand what is expected of him. Let's look at some examples:

> William, a child with Asperger's Syndrome, likes baseball. He frequently puts on his baseball glove, gets his ball, and approaches a peer. William does not understand that the peer may be engaged in doing something else. Instead of asking the peer to play ball with him, William throws the ball at the other child. When the peer turns away from William, he gets upset.

An appropriate social story for William might include how to ask others to play with him.

> *Amanda, a child with autism, frequently screams when she wants to watch a video on television, and if her sister is watching something else she screams and falls on the floor. Instead of asking if she might watch a video, she tries to kick her sister.*

Amanda would benefit from a social story about learning to ask others to let her have a turn or learning how to ask her sister to stop watching a video and let her watch television.

Once you determine which social skill you want to focus on, it is time to start writing a social story. As you begin to write, keep in mind that social stories should be short, written in the first person (I, we), in the present tense ("ask" not "will ask") and designed to help your child learn how to act in a social situation. A sample social story appears on the following page.

According to Carol Gray, author and developer of "social stories," it is important to include sentences that have clear directions so your child knows how to act. When your child becomes more socially competent, you can write stories with fewer directions so your child can learn to decide for himself how he should respond or react.

On the next page is a social story written for William, the child who enjoys baseball. Remember, his problem is that he does not know how to ask other children to play catch with him.

*I like to play baseball. I have a new ball and glove. I want Tom to play catch with me. Sometimes, Tom is having fun playing with his cars. When I want Tom to play with me, I tap him on the shoulder. I say, "Tom, would you play baseball with me?" I try not to just throw the ball at Tom when I want him to play with me. I try to learn to ask Tom to play ball.*

The following pages outline a few ideas and strategies to help your child develop social skills. These strategies are:

- Hi! My Name Is ____.
- Telephone Talk: Following Simple Directions
- Learning to Say "Thank You"
- Three Breaths Away (A Strategy for Calming Down)

## Hi! My Name Is ____.

Use this strategy to help your child learn to introduce himself and say "Hello" and "Goodbye" to a new person. This strategy is most effective when your child is relaxed and not anxious.

**Materials**
None

**What to Do**
1. Teach your child the process involved in meeting someone new:
   - Walk up to the person you want to meet.
   - Stand one arm-length away. (**Note:** Practice where to stand, because your child may find it difficult to know how close or how far back to stand.)
   - Look at the face of the person you want to meet. Smile.
   - Say, "Hi, my name is ____ (fill in the child's name)."
   - Wait!
   - Say, "I like to ____ (fill in something the child likes to do)."
   - Wait!
   - Say, "Bye."
   - Wait! Walk away.
2. Go through each step, one at a time. Ask your child to do each step right after you model it for him.
3. Provide opportunities for the child to practice. Ask other family members if they would like to pretend they are meeting someone new.
4. Review the steps often.
5. At first, the child may not be able to remember all the steps. If he forgets, remind him gently by saying, "Next, you ____."

## Telephone Talk: Following Simple Directions

Use this strategy to teach your child how to follow simple directions. This works best when the child is not upset or not already involved in another activity.

### Materials

Two Styrofoam cups, string or yarn, scissors (adult only)

### What to Do

1. Using the scissors, make a small hole in the bottom of each cup (adult-only step). Put a piece of string or yarn through each hole and tie a large knot.
2. Tell your child that you are going to play a game with her. Place one cup to your ear and hold it there.
3. Say something to your child, such as, "Touch your nose."
4. Continue to tell your child to do something simple, such as, "Wave at me" or "Turn around once."
5. After you have given a few simple directions, see if your child will give you a command.

### Helpful Hints

■ Tell your child that this is like a real phone because one person receives a message and other person responds.

■ After your child is more familiar with the game, suggest that she play it with other children.

■ As your child learns to follow one-step directions, try two-step directions. For example, "Touch your nose and then wave at me."

## Learning to Say "Thank You"

Use this strategy to teach your child to say or sign "thank you" when someone helps him.

**Materials**
None

thank you

**What to Do**

1. Decide whether you are going to encourage your child to say or sign "thank you," or to do both.
2. If you are going to use the sign, demonstrate how to use it. The sign for "thank you" is made by touching your lips with the tips of the fingers of your right hand. Move your hand away from your face, palms upward. Smile. If you use two hands with this sign, it means, "Thank you very much."
3. Tell your child that you are going to show him what to do when someone does something for him. Explain that saying or signing "thank you" lets the other person know that you like what that person did for you.
4. Recite the following chant for your child:

   *When you like what others do*
   *Smile at them* (smile) *and say, "Thank you!"*

5. Use the chant frequently with your child.
6. Model saying and/or using the sign for "thank you" when anyone in your family does something for someone else.

**Helpful Hints**

■ Send a letter to school telling your child's teacher that you are working on saying, "thank you." (Include a copy of the chant for them to use at school.)
■ Praise your child when he says or signs, "thank you."

## Three Breaths Away (A Strategy for Calming Down)

**Note:** Deep breathing is a technique that can help your child calm himself.

**Materials**
None

**What to Do**
1. Tell your child you are going to show him something he can do when he is becoming stressed by people or situations.
2. Tell him that it involves breathing. First say, "I want you to breathe with me. We will take a big breath, hold it, and then see if we can blow all the breath out."
3. Practice together. Take a deep breath. Hold it. Blow out all the air.
4. Next say, "I will bring my hands together (place your hands in front of you like you are going to clap)."
5. Then say, "Now, I will put my hands down and take another breath."
6. Repeat this process, until you have done it three times.
7. Say to your child, "Next time you think you are getting upset, come to me and we will breathe."
8. Try to provide opportunities for your child to practice this technique.
9. Remember, if your child can focus on breathing before he gets too upset, the strategy has a much better chance of being successful.

**Helpful Hints**
- It may take several times before your child understands what you are asking him to do.
- Don't give up; keep trying. Once your child learns to do this strategy, it can greatly reduce his number of outbursts.

## For More Information

Abrams, P. & L. Henriques. 2004. *The autistic spectrum: Parent's daily helper.* Berkeley, CA: Ulysses Press.

Bareket, R. 2006. *Playing it right! Social skills activities for parents and teachers of young children with autism spectrum disorders, including asperger syndrome and autism.* Shawnee Mission, KS: Autism Asperger Publishing Company.

White, A. Gray, C. & McAndrew, S. 2005 *My social stories book.* London: Jessica Kingsley Publishers.

Willis, C. 2009. *Creating inclusive learning environments for young children: What to do on Monday morning.* Thousand Oaks, CA: Corwin Publishing.

## Key Terms

**Egocentric**: Self-absorbed, people who believe the world revolves around them.

**Social story**: A strategy, designed by Carol Gray, where stories are used to help children with autism learn social interaction skills in the context of a story.

**Socially avoidant:** A type of social challenge characterized by a child who tries to escape social situations.

**Socially awkward:** A type of social challenge characterized by a child who does not understand the give-and-take nature of a social interaction.

**Socially competent:** By definition, a socially competent child has developed strong interpersonal communication skills, knows how to form relationships with peers, and understands the value of appropriately interacting with others.

**Socially indifferent:** A type of social challenge characterized by a child who is indifferent to social situations.

# Chapter 8

# Encouraging Your Child to Play

*Phillip can play. In fact, he does play. He just does it in his own way, and he has fun. Shouldn't play be about having fun?*
*—Karon, the mother of Phillip*

## How Does My Child's Autism Change the Way He Plays?

Play is a valuable and fun way to learn. It helps children develop relationships with others, learn how to solve problems, express emotions, and use their imagination to create new experiences and explore the world around them. Play is the main vehicle through which children learn to get along with others and socialize; it is how children experiment and solve problems in their world. Play skills develop as children begin to experience new activities and explore new environments. The solitary play of a toddler, with experience, develops into the interactive, reciprocal play of a preschool-age child.

In general, the stages of play start when children begin to explore their world by manipulating and experimenting with objects that interest them. Later, children incorporate objects into their play, such as placing a block on top of another block or putting a plastic spoon beside a bowl. The next stage of play is when children substitute one object for another, such as picking up a block and pretending it is a camera. This leads to imaginative play or pretend play.

## The Qualities of Play

- Play is a fun and joyful experience.
- When children are actively involved in an experience, they are playing.
- Play is something children do because they want to, not because they have to do it.
- Play has no real agenda, except what children want it to be.
- When children learn to use symbols, such as when a cardboard box becomes a jet plane, they are playing.
- Play is how children learn the rules of socialization.

Children with autism do not follow a typical pattern when they play. Because many children with autism become obsessed with objects in non-typical ways and do not socialize easily, their play is not as socially interactive as that of their peers. In addition, many children with autism are often repetitive in their movements, have communication issues, and are not interested in the world around them, which makes it challenging to encourage children with autism to play with others. Although children with autism may manipulate objects or engage in some form of experimental play, it is usually very different from that of their peers.

While children with autism tend to be somewhat involved with materials and objects that involve the senses, they often show a marked preference for only one type of play material. For example, Sam will build a road for his cars but he only uses square blocks and he only plays with red cars. Also, since children with autism are usually very literal, they do not always understand or show any desire to participate in symbolic or pretend play. In addition, make-believe and imaginative play, especially if it involves role play or interaction with others, is very uncommon.

It is very difficult for children with autism to understand the social relationships involved in playing successfully with others. Even if they are interested in such interactions, most children with autism do not know how to engage themselves in a play activity with someone else. For this reason, they become even more socially isolated. While their peers are learning to build relationships in play groups and play activities, children with autism are often left sitting alone, absorbed in a favorite toy. Jerome, for example, enjoys making a collage out of bits of fabric, string, and colored paper. However, if you ask him to make a kite with a peer, he turns his back on you and walks away.

# What Can I Do to Encourage My Child to Play?

Before you can encourage your child to play, it is helpful to spend time observing him as he plays. Use a version of the chart on pages 144–145 to make notes that will help you determine what interests your child most. Structuring play around your child's interests will increase the chances of positive play interactions and will make him more likely to show an interest in what is going on.

## Play Observations

| Questions to Ask | How Does My Child Play? | Examples You Observe |
|---|---|---|
| Does he prefer a toy or an object? | ■ What does he do with it?<br>■ Does he play?<br>■ Does he just watch while it moves?<br>■ Does he just sit and stare at the object? | |
| What activity does he seem to repeat? | ■ How does he act when he is repeating the activity?<br>■ Does it have more than one step?<br>■ Will he let others engage in the activity with him? | |
| What materials does he use most often? | ■ Is his preference for color or size?<br>■ Does he prefer one texture over another?<br>■ How does he respond when you introduce something new, such as a new toy? | |
| What does he do when he plays with an object or toy? | ■ Will he engage in multiple activities with the same toy?<br>■ Will he let others share the toy with him?<br>■ Does he play appropriately with the toy or does he just repeat a movement over and over? | |

**Play Observations** (cont'd.)

| Questions to Ask | How Does My Child Play? | Examples You Observe |
|---|---|---|
| Does he have a collection or need to have an object with him when he plays? | ■ Will he put aside his desired object when something new is introduced? | |
| If he does engage in pretend play, is there a theme he prefers? | ■ Does he use the same theme (pretending to be a doctor or a firefighter) every time he plays?<br>■ Will he assign themes to other activities? | |
| Does he play with others? Who? | ■ If he does play with others, who does he play with most?<br>■ Will he play with other children or just adults? | |

# How Do I Use What I Have Observed?

After observing how your child plays and what he prefers to play with, it will be easier to plan activities that focus on his interests. Make sure your child has time to play with preferred objects and is not under stress to stop or share the toy until he is ready. Once your child has played with the preferred item for a few minutes, encourage him to try something new by putting the new toy beside him and walking away. Don't take away the preferred toy; after a few minutes, return and ask if your child would like to play with the new toy.

# Ideas and Activities for Encouraging Your Child to Play

When trying to encourage your child, keep the following in mind:

- Focus on the interests of your child.
- Make interactions with others as natural as possible.
- Recognize that your child may have difficulty adjusting to new play situations and new play materials.
- Explain activities that involve more than one step and provide picture cues to help your child know what to do next.
- Allow your child to leave a play activity if it becomes overwhelming.
- Honor your child's need to play alone; he may not be ready to play in with other children.
- Avoid upsetting your child; let him know ahead of time that it will soon be time to stop playing, so that he has time to accept that there will be a change.

## General Suggestions for Teaching Play Strategies

Use the following suggestions before selecting a strategy to help your child learn to play:

- Introduce one new toy or activity at a time. Too much change can be overwhelming.
- If you are teaching your child to do something for the first time, break it down into a few simple steps.
- Show your child each step. Then, ask him to repeat it after you.
- Start off with very short periods of structured play. Then, make the time longer as your child learns to tolerate the activity.

- Talk about the activity. Be animated and use a happy approach by saying such things as, "Wow, I just love rolling the ball to you!" or, "You built that tower so high, isn't this fun?"
- If your child is prone to a self-stimulatory activity, such as hand flapping or hitting himself, try to find an activity that uses his hands in other ways.
- When teaching a new skill, use your child's name and tell him what will happen.
- Next, show him or model the steps in the activity, and encourage your child to try the activity on his own.
- Make sure every play activity is fun and rewarding for your child. Remember, the main reason children play is because it is fun!

---

The following pages outline a few ideas and strategies to help your child play with other children. These strategies are:

- Which Toy Should I Use?
- Give and Take—Learning Reciprocity
- Same Old, Same Old, Same Old—Introducing a New Toy
- May I Play, Too? Asking to Join a Game or Activity
- Time to Stop—Putting Away Toys and Activities

## Which Toy Should I Use?

Use this strategy to help you determine the toys your child needs to learn and grow, and which toys your child prefers to play with.

### Materials

Toys that interest your child

### What to Do

1. Consider the age of your child, his social skills, and how well he communicates with others.
2. Select a toy based on your child's development and needs as well as your goals and objectives for him. (The chart on the next page contains general guidelines for selecting toys.)
3. Trial-and-error can be the best tool. Introduce a toy and see if your child seems to take an interest in it. If he does not, try something else.
4. Be creative; sometimes a large box can quickly become a wonderful pretend airplane or a tunnel.
5. Because some children with autism enjoy crawling in and around things, try making a simple obstacle course using common materials, such as chairs, tables, or large therapy balls.

### Helpful Hints

- Your agenda and your child's preferences may not match. Be flexible enough to change your plans if your child wants to do something else.
- As your child begins to communicate more, introduce games with rules. Start with matching games and move up to more traditional games, such as Candyland or Hi-Ho! Cherry–O.

## Guidelines for Selecting Toys

| Type and General Purpose of Toy | Examples |
| --- | --- |
| Cause-and-effect toys or toys that require an action by your child, such as pushing a button or pulling a leverJack-in-the-box | Flashlight<br>Simple switch-operated toys such as a tape recorder<br>See-N-Say toys |
| Toys that are related to visual-spatial needs | Puzzles with knobs<br>Stacking rings<br>Nesting cups<br>Shape-sorting toys |
| Toys that aid in construction or building | Blocks of various shapes and sizes<br>Building toys, such<br>Stringing beads<br>Snap-together toys |
| Toys that encourage an exchange between two people | Small hand-held toys such as balls<br>Blowing bubbles<br>Small moving toys such as cars, trucks, and airplanes |
| Sensory materials that encourage creativity | Art materials, paint, glue, scraps of cloth or paper, art paper, crayons<br>String or yarn |
| "Let's pretend" toys | Puppets<br>Realistic-looking toys that represent things such as food, clothes, and so on<br>Dress-up clothes including hats, shoes, and jewelry |

## Give and Take—Learning Reciprocity

Initially, this strategy involves just you and your child; later, it can be expanded to include other children. The strategy works best when your child is relaxed.

### Materials

Small hand-held toy, such as a ball or car

### What to Do

1. Sit facing your child. You will need to sit close to her. Later, as she learns what to do, you can move back.
2. Hold up the item you want to exchange (ball, car, doll, and so on). Make sure the toy is in your child's line of vision. Smile and show lots of interest in the toy.
3. Use your child's name and the toy's name in a sentence. For example, "Sarah, look, I have a doll."
4. Repeat Step 3 until your child glances at the doll. When she does, look at the doll and place it in her hand.
5. Identify the doll as your child's. For example, say, "Sarah's doll," pause, and see if your child will hold the doll.
6. Gently take the doll back, and say, "My doll." Place your free hand on your chest and gently tap it a couple of times as a cue that says, "mine."
7. Repeat the process, using the same words each time. Remember to pause to give your child an opportunity to take the doll.
8. After a few times of taking the doll back, wait, and extend your hand, to see if your child will place the doll into your hand.

## Same Old, Same Old, Same Old— Introducing a New Toy

Use this strategy to introduce a new toy when your child is relaxed and having fun. It is less effective when your child is over-stimulated by the environment, or when he is tired.

### Materials
A new toy that you want to introduce to your child

### What to Do
1. Before your child becomes involved in play, place the new toy on a table and cover it loosely with a piece of cloth.
2. Tell your child that you have hidden something under the cloth on the table and you want to see if he can figure out what it is.
3. Sit down with your child in front of the hidden toy. Lightly touch the toy without removing the blanket. Make a comment, such as, "Hmmm...this feels soft" or "Listen, I think this toy makes a noise."
4. Encourage your child to explore the toy without looking under the cloth.
5. Continue to explore the toy. Say things like, "Do you think it is a ____?"
6. After a few minutes, ask your child to guess what is hidden under the cloth. Pause, and wait for him to answer.
7. Lift the cloth with your child and say, "Oh look, it is a ____ (fill in the name of the toy)."

### Helpful Hints
- Your child may be hesitant to explore new toys. Think of creative ways to direct his attention to the new toy.
- After you have uncovered the toy, ask your child to play with it.

## May I Play, Too? Asking to Join a Game or Activity

This strategy works best when your child is developmentally ready to participate in joint-play activities. This strategy is effective with children who are high-functioning, such as children with Asperger's Syndrome.

### Materials

Four index cards, glue, pictures showing: *walk, stop, listen* (ears with cupped hand), and "*?*"

### What to Do

1. Glue one picture on each index card. Then, lay the cards out in the following order: *walk, stop, listen,* and "*?*".

2. Tell your child that you are going to show him the steps to follow when he wants to join in a game or activity.

3. Go over each step and point to the card. For example, say, "First, you walk up to where other children are playing." Point to the card showing *walk.* "Next, you stop and watch." Point to the card with *stop* on it. "Then, you listen," and "Last of all, you ask a question. You ask, 'May I play, too?'"

4. Tell your child that you will practice each step with him. Go over each step several times, and model exactly what to do.

5. If possible, ask another child to help you demonstrate the rules for joining in a game.

## Time to Stop—Putting Away Toys and Activities

This strategy is most effective if you give your child ample notice that it will soon be time to clean up. If you use this routine consistently, it will be easier for your child to learn to help put away his toys.

**Materials**

Small, hand-held bell or service bell

**What to Do**

1. Tell your child that when you ring the bell two times, it means that it will soon be time to put away his toys.
2. After you ring the bell two times, wait approximately three to four minutes and ring the bell once again. Explain that this single ring means it is time to clean up.
3. Teach your child the clean-up song, sung to the tune of "Here We Go 'Round the Mulberry Bush."

   *This is the way we clean up our toys,*
   *Clean up our toys, clean up our toys.*
   *This is the way we clean up our toys*
   *Every single day!*

4. Tell your child that after you ring the bell once, you will start to hum the song. When he hears you humming, he must stop and finish what he is doing.
5. Sing the song and invite your child to sing along with you as he picks up the toys.
6. Go over all the steps and practice what he is to do: Two rings means a few more minutes to play, one ring means time to finish up, humming means it is time to pick up toys, and singing means it is time to pick up toys.

## For More Information

Gammeltoft, L. & Nordenhof, M. 2007. *Autism, play, and social interaction.* London: Jessica Kingsley.

Moor, J. 2005. *Playing, laughing, and learning with children on the autism spectrum.* London: Jessica Kingsley.

Moor, J. 2008. *Playing, laughing and learning with children on the autism spectrum: A practical resource of play ideas for parents and carers.* London: Jessica Kingsley.

Sonders, S.A. 2003. *Giggle time: Establishing the social connection.* London: Jessica Kingsley.

## Key Terms

**Imaginative play:** Play activities that involve using imagination.

**Parallel play:** When one child plays near or beside another child and may even share some of the same toys, but the children do not play together in a reciprocal fashion.

**Personal space:** The space in which someone feels comfortable, his or her comfort zone.

**Pretend play:** Make-believe play.

**Reciprocal play:** Direct play with a partner when children playing interact with each other.

**Socialization:** The ability to get along with others.

**Solitary play:** Playing alone or play that does not involve others.

**Symbolic play:** Using one object or toy to represent another, such as pretending a square block is a camera or that a cardboard box is a jet plane.

# References and Resources

Baker, B. L., & A.J. Brightman. 2003. *Steps to independence: Teaching everyday skills to children with special needs.* Baltimore, MD: Paul H. Brookes.

Baker, Jed E. 2003. Social skills training: *For children and adolescents with Asperger syndrome and social-communication problems.* Shawnee Mission, KS: Autism Asperger Publishing Company.

Bondy, A. & L. Frost. 2002. *A picture's worth: PECS and other visual communication strategies in autism.* Bethesda, MD: Woodbine House.

Buie, T. 2005. *Treating autism in children: Neuro-gastroenterology and autism.* A paper presented at Harvard University: Learning and the Brain Conference (12th Conference), Cambridge, MA.

Cohen, S. 2002. *Targeting autism: What we know, don't know, and can do to help young children with autism and related disorders.* Berkley, CA: University of California Press.

Fouse, B. & M. Wheeler. 1997. *A treasure chest of behavioral strategies for individuals with autism.* Arlington, TX: Future Horizons.

Gutstein, S. E. & R. Sheely. 2002. *Relationship development intervention with young children: Social and emotional development activities for Asperger syndrome, autism, PDD and NLD.* London: Jessica Kingsley.

Hanbury, M. 2005. *Educating pupils with autistic spectrum disorders: A practical guide.* London: Paul Chapman.

Isbell, C. & R. Isbell. 2005. *The inclusive learning center book for preschool children with special needs.* Beltsville, MD: Gryphon House.

Janzen, J. E. 2003. *Understanding the nature of autism: A guide to the autism spectrum disorders.* San Antonio, TX: Therapy Skill Builders.

Janzen, J. E., & Therapy Skills Builders. 2000. *Autism: Facts and strategies for parents.* New York: Elsevier Science.

Johnson, M. D., & S.H. Corden. 2004. *Beyond words: The successful inclusion of a child with autism.* Knoxville, TN: Merry Pace Press.

Kluth, P. 2003. *You're going to love this kid!: Teaching students with autism in the inclusive classroom.* Baltimore, MD: Paul H. Brookes.

Kranowitz, C.S. 2003. *The out-of-sync child has fun: Safe activities for home and school—sensory-motor, appropriate, fun, and easy.* New York: The Berkeley Publishing Group.

Kranowitz, C.S. 2005. *The out-of-sync child: Recognizing and coping with sensory integration dysfunction.* New York: Penguin.

Leaf, R. (Ed.), & J. McEachin. 1999. *A work in progress: Behavior management strategies and a curriculum for intensive behavioral treatment of autism.* New York: Autism Partnership.

MacDonald, L. 2000. *Learning interrupted: Maladaptive behavior in the classroom.* Retrieved from http://www.mugsy.org

McClannahan, L. E., & P.J. Krantz. 1998. *Activity schedules for children with autism: Teaching independent behavior.* Bethesda, MD: Woodbine House.

Murray-Slutsky, C. & B.A. Paris. 2001. *Exploring the spectrum of autism and pervasive developmental disorders: Intervention strategies.* New York: Elsevier Science.

Schiller, P. 2002. *Start smart! Building brain power in the early years.* Beltsville, MD: Gryphon House.

Scott, J., C. Clark, & M.P. Brady. 1999. *Students with autism: Characteristics and instructional programming for special educators.* Belmont, CA: Wadsworth Publishing.

Siegel, B. 2003. *Helping children with autism learn: Treatment approaches for parents and professionals.* New York: Oxford University Press.

Sigman, M., & L. Capps. 1997. *Children with autism: A developmental perspective.* Cambridge, MA: Harvard University Press.

Sinclair, J. 1993. *Don't mourn for us.* Autism Network International Newsletter, 1(3).

Small, M. & L. Kontente. 2003. *Everyday solutions: A practical guide for families of children with autism spectrum disorders.* Shawnee Mission, KS: Autism Asperger Publishing Company.

Sonders, S.A. 2002. *Giggle time: Establishing the social connection: a program to develop the communication skills of children with autism, Asperger's Syndrome, and PDD.* London: Jessica Kingsley.

Strock, M. 2004. *Autism spectrum disorders (Pervasive Developmental Disorders).* Bethesda, MD: National Institute of Mental Health, National Institutes of Health, U.S. Department of Health and Human Services. (NIH Publication No. NIH-04-5511)

Sussman, F. 1999. *More than words: Helping parents promote communication and social skills in young children with autism spectrum disorder.* Toronto: The Hanen Centre.

Wall, K. 2004. *Autism and early years practice: A guide for early years professionals, teachers, and parents.* London: Paul Chapman.

Weatherby, A.M., & B. Prizant. 2001. *Autism spectrum disorders: A transactional developmental perspective,* Vol. 9. Baltimore, MD: Paul H. Brookes.

Williams, D. 1996. *Autism: An inside-out approach: An innovative look at the mechanics of autism and its developmental cousins.* London: Jessica Kingsley.

Willis, C. 1998. *Language development: A key to lifelong learning.* Child Care Information Exchange, 121, 63-65.

Willis, C. 1999. *Brain research implications for caregivers and teachers.* The Viewpoint. The Virginia Association for Early Childhood Education, 2, 1-3.

Wolfberg, P. 2003. *Peer play and the autism spectrum.* Shawnee Mission, KS: Autism, Asperger Publishing Company.

Yee, C.E. (n.d.). *How to know if it's sensory/What to do?* Retrieved August 2, 2005, from http://www.autism-pdd.net